THE
Playbook
OF A
Mindset Snob

BIANCA WISE

For permission requests, write to the publisher, addressed "Attention:
Permissions Coordinator," 205 N. Michigan Avenue, Suite #810,
Chicago, IL 60601. 13th & Joan books may be purchased for
educational, business or sales promotional use. For information,
please email the Sales Department at sales@13thandjoan.com.

Printed in the U. S. A.

First Printing, November 2023.

Library of Congress Cataloging-in-Publication
Data has been applied for.

ISBN: 978-1-953156-97-6

ACKNOWLEDGEMENTS

To my mother, who passed away in 2005 as I was just getting started in my fire department career. It's funny when you connect the dots with how you came to be the type of person you are. My mother was straight savage. She worked for the Federal Bureau of Investigation (FBI) for 25 years. I would witness her get up every day at four o' clock in the morning to take the commute from Baltimore to DC.. She would leave with her business suit and briefcase, because she was a boss. Even as a little girl, I recognized she was a powerful woman, and I have been carrying her boss spirit since birth.

I want to acknowledge my older brother. He has always covered me as a young girl growing up in the inner-city of Baltimore. He helped me gain my street knowledge and was the strongest male figure in my life who provided protection and guidance. When it comes to my brother, he has been here since day one. He has been the consistent one who when I tell him about all the crazy stuff I am planning to do, he is like, "Okay, do it."

To my husband, who supported me 100000% when I came and told him 3 months before we were due to be married that I was leaving the fire department and starting a business. It did not shake him one bit. He was like, "Okay, go ahead and do it." He supports me unconditionally through this wild journey.

I also have a very intimate group of male and female friends from my high school years to my fire department tenure, and extracurricular activities who support and love me through all my craziness. They are my tribe of people who are always cheerleading for me. They will come through when they have no idea what I am going through or when I need a little bit of motivation or cheering up. They come through at the right moment and help me to keep going. They love me for me and I love them for that. You know who you are.

PREFACE

I have always been a free-spirited person, so I make these bold decisions.

I decided to write this book because of my journey in life. I have always been a very bold, lively individual. When I say bold, I make decisions that are often misunderstood by everyone else. It starts with me joining the fire department. From where I come, who does that? It's just this unconventional mentality of mine. I have always been a free-spirited person. A lot of times you're underestimated and overlooked, but you know innately through your self-confidence and self-belief that you are going to excel. So that was the fire department. I didn't come from the background of people with fire department experience, but I got into the career and excelled to the point where I advanced and made history by being the first Black woman ever promoted in that department.

Then I make another bold decision to leave and move on to something else. To wake up one day and determine to leave a career of 20 years to go into business ownership is life-changing. Again from the outside looking in, people were confused. Even me. I was like, *"What did I just do?"* But by tapping back into that confidence, within three years of leaving my career, I built a seven-figure organization that is still growing. I got to a point where I understood that I have a platform where other people are watching me. There are other people at a crossroad where they know they are destined for more in life. Still, they may be stuck. I think they will find my story to be inspirational.

This book is for people who do not need convincing. It's for the people who already know they just need a little push, a little inspiration, some evidence for them to say, *"Okay, let me just do it because I understand everything that is being said here. I am living it. I just needed to see or hear from someone else."* I have read many books about mindset, and I will honestly say they have been the catalyst to push me forward. I am confident my book can inspire others..

Despite my individuality and my confidence on the surface level, I had a hard time writing this book because I had to wrap my mind around the audacity I adopted to believe I should be the one writing this book. Many people write books like this, people who have spent years in the thick of things–scholars, thought leaders, philosophers who have done the research. Here I am a simple woman from Baltimore, Maryland, who just took a chance with her life to make a book and to spread what she learned through her own experiences. I had a few bouts with imposter syndrome, like *"Who am I? Why should people listen to me?"* I understood that just like anyone else, I had something to say. My experience is unique like everyone else's and if my voice can help one person, then I have accomplished my job. If I am being honest, I want this to impact millions of people.

EPIGRAPH

Your life is in your own hands. Do not let the realities of the world hold you down. If you want to accomplish things in this world, stay focused, stay positive. Make the choice to change and the world will change around you.

CONTENTS

INTRODUCTION

*"I silently committed that by my 10th anniversary in the
fire department, I would make rank and become an officer.
I wrote it on this dirty sticky note and put it in my locker.
I taped it to the back of my locker to see it daily."*

We, as human beings, struggle on a daily basis. We have things or
circumstances in our lives that drive us to the point of wanting
to throw in the towel or punch a wall. Especially as an adult, with the
mounting distractions at our disposal and the societal pressure to be a
certain way, life is daunting, confusing, and overbearing.

Think about this for a second: You look at Instagram, and what do
you see? People are throwing around money. Beautiful women who
appear to have perfect bodies with no imperfections are the norm.
Then you look at yourself in the mirror and see cellulite while you're
living with your mom and have no real career prospects. Then you fall
into this pit of negativity, insecurity, and depression. It's a crazy cycle
we have created for ourselves, that for some just cannot be overcome.

However, it is that exact mentality that is keeping you down, that
prevents you from becoming the authentic person you were meant
to be. You have allowed the world–or fake world–other people live
in to influence your way of life. You have not created your own path,
but instead seek to live someone else's life or follow in someone else's
footsteps. You realize that it is not as easy as you thought. I was there

before. I was living this monotonous life, filled with a repeating cycle that was not fulfilling me. I was adopting the mindset and career path others set out for me instead of doing what I wanted. It led to many years of wasting my time on something that was not fulfilling me and was internally breaking me. I knew I needed to break away or spend the next 25 years of my life as a broken woman.

I first started with my mindset and creating an understanding of what I wanted in life. Once that was done, it was full-scale ahead from there. I spent every day working toward my goal, and I did not let other people get in my head about what was possible and what was not. I wanted to get a promotion, and I did. I wanted to open a business, and I did. I wanted to open a seven-figure earning business, and I did. All the while, I had people around–whether friends, family, or social influencers–telling me how it was impossible. Because of this external reason, I could not do this or that was not what women do or, more specifically, what Black women did. Each time I looked at those people with a smile and said "I appreciate your concern, but I am going to do this, and it will happen." Now I would be lying to you if I made it seem easy because it definitely was not. Changing your mindset, getting a promotion, running a business: None of this was easy, but I was determined and I was focused. I also decided to create an environment that promoted growth and positivity. I minimized my time with people, places, and things that did not serve me or provide value. I did not allow other people's influence to affect me. I fundamentally changed my entire life as much as I could to be a center of health, wealth, and positivity.

Now that I have gone through the journey and experienced the bumps, I feel it is my obligation to spread my message to you all. At first glance, I don't come off as Gary Vee or Eric Thomas, and I am not trying to be them. I am just trying to be myself and give the advice and tips that best helped me reach my goals of becoming the first African American woman promoted to lieutenant in the history of the Baltimore County Fire Department and coming to terms with being destined for even greater opportunities. I made the difficult choice to leave my career to start a business and then grew that business to seven figures within 2 1/2 years. I am not an expert by far, but I am a woman with a story that

I hope will inspire others to pursue what they want in life and grow into the person they want to be, breaking free of the chains holding some of you back from reaching our full potential.

In this book, I will show you the mindset you need to have to be successful, what you need to focus on in life, and how to build an environment built for success instead of mediocrity. Some of it may seem challenging initially, but some of the core concepts you get from this book will be all you need. How you apply them in your life is up to you as an individual. What you see is what I have done and what I recommend, but feel free to take what I have done and adjust to your life as you see fit. We all want to be successful and be more in life, but to do that requires a level of sacrifice and work. So if you are willing to strap up your bootstraps and do what needs to be done while having a good time along the way, this is the book for you.

PILLAR 1

CONFIDENCE

*"Life's journey seems to throw hands at times, but
it's your confidence leveling up."*

THE STORY

Confidence is where we operate and believe in our abilities and qualities. It's self-assurance that we are in control of who we are.

I'm a person who loves to give. I love to help people, be resourceful, and be a positive beacon in the world. It comes naturally, and I think it affected me early on in life when people didn't reciprocate that behavior. When I was younger, I expected that people would treat me the way I treat them, and when you run into experiences where that doesn't happen, it becomes disappointing to deal with. It was especially difficult when friends and family let me down because I had a different expectation from them versus just a stranger. If I go out and help a stranger, I don't have too much expectation because I don't know anything about them. Still, when someone who is supposed to care about me doesn't reciprocate the love I have for them, my expectation is kind of shot. Then I realize, "*Well damn,*" like I do all of this for people and it wasn't reciprocated. It leaves you in this place where you do not trust people, nor do you trust yourself because at the end of the day, you decided to help people who did not come to your aid.

As I've gotten older, I've realized that you can't have expectations of anybody. I have to understand–and I'm just making that decision to do it–that the expectation is not that people will reciprocate in any way. It could be as simple as taking time to talk and help me through a situation. It might be months later, I'll call them, trying to pick their brain, and they are just unavailable or don't return my calls or respond to text messages. It makes me feel *"Well damn, every time they call me, I'll pick up the phone or if I'm unable to pick up the phone, I'll make sure I call them back."* Still, I have to hunt this person down to get just a couple of minutes with them. As I said, there are times when it has put me in spaces where I have to come back and realize that, *"OK, their behavior does not affect me or have an effect on me."* Their lack of applause or acknowledgment of things that I have done or accomplished does not take away from the value of what I've done. I am in control of my value, and I do not allow people who take from me to have any control over me. Instead, I weed out those who do not belong and surround myself with people who want the best and give me their all in a relationship, as I do for them.

THE LESSON

Confidence can be built by seeking out inspiration that may often come from a person you don't know, by searching for a mentorship, or educating yourself. The popular saying is that *"Knowledge is power,"* but that's not entirely true. The *application* of knowledge is power. You can read and learn about something all day, but until you take that next step, until it becomes an action, the information is pointless and just rattling in your mind doing nothing significant.

When those first results show up, you're like, *"Oh man, OK, I did that. I can do it again."* Once you have accomplished that first goal and gotten the desired results, it becomes easier just to try again. Educating yourself and being inspired by people, whether they are dead or alive, can put you on the right path.

Social media gives us front-row seats to super successful people, giving us insight into their techniques and how they became who they are or access to their Ted Talks or self-help courses. If you do not find a mentor, surround yourself with other confident people because energy is contagious. You have to be coachable because today, everybody thinks they are a chief and that they know everything. We have all these life coaches, we have all these million-dollar entrepreneurs on Instagram teaching us how to build this and start that. But you have to be conscious and remain conscious about the people you surround yourself with, and conscious about who you are aligning yourself with as well. That goes back to you being mindful of the communities and people who you align yourself with. You need to do your research and ensure you know what you are getting into because there is a lot of fraud. If you use discernment, you can pick up on what's not authentic very quickly.

When you align with people in spaces where you're trying to climb or where you want to be, listen to them, take what resonates, and then throw the rest away. The one thing that successful people always say is *"Success leaves clues."* If you get into a room with very successful people–people who are in places where you're striving to be–and they are willing to take the time to talk to you, do not disregard what they are saying. Don't think you know better than what they're saying, or that your friend's baby mama did it this way, which turns people off. You're not able to elevate if you're not coachable. People will tend not to want to help you. We can all learn something from somebody, but lessons go unheard if you are not paying attention.

Remember, though, that confidence can be broken with words and doubt instilled in you by other people. That's why it's important to work on those key things that help you stay focused and grounded. You're doing the work that you need to do for yourself. As humans, we want to feel like we belong or are a part of something. That's all fine and good, but we can't allow that to make or break us. If you step into a room with a stranger and within yourself, you don't have the confidence to understand that *"I am supposed to be in this room,"* then you can become broken. It is not necessarily that the people in the room did anything specific to you but because you don't feel confident in your skin, simply being around them makes you uncomfortable and scared. Then it shows on your face or through your mannerisms, and things take an even deeper nose dive.

If you are in an atmosphere of low self-esteem, you must get out of there because energy is contagious. You have to have a sense of focus because we have a herd mentality, and it's security for survival. We want to be in our tribes and our herd. That's where we feel safe with everything, even our thoughts. Somebody can put an opinion out on Facebook and have 100,000 people regurgitating the thought. It's like, *"Well, did you ever stop and think about what they're saying before you made the decision to agree with their perspective? Or did you take a moment to think for yourself to confidently come to agreeance of someone else's thoughts?"* But its difficult to stand up and speak for yourself because you don't want to be looked at as the person who is going against the grain. From firsthand experience I can tell you that you can fake it for a minute but after a while, you have to make your choice. Be true to yourself through all of your thoughts, actions, or behaviors, or just conform and lose yourself completely. If you show up in an environment that's not serving you or aligning with you, it will push you out. Either people will act weird around you or you won't grow or be nurtured. You'll have a characteristic change in yourself and then there you go, not being motivated and feeling sadness. We don't understand why, but we tend to blame it on our circumstances or anyone we can find to shift blame to. *"My job is so demanding,"* or *"Susan on the 5th floor doesn't like me"* or *"My boss is an idiot."* It's like, *"OK, no, you have to stop and acknowledge your role."* It becomes your choice to keep showing up in an environment that does not serve you, so you must get out or shift. However, there is another option. You can decide to stay in your current situation temporarily to get all you need to help you get to your next level and better adapt to future situations.

The actions that irritate us from other people are a reflection of things that we need to work on ourselves. People will take their lack of self-confidence and reflect that on to someone else and, as I said, label others as being arrogant or whatever and then tell them that they need to humble themselves. Honestly, how do you have the audacity to tell somebody else to humble themselves? Where do you get that authority? That's always been a question for me: Who are you? Let's say you are observing someone who you feel is coming across as arrogant. Back in the day, the elders would say, *"You're getting too big for your britches,"* *"You're smelling yourself,"* or *"You're on a high horse."* I would hear all these little things from my elders growing up, but then you get to a certain age and self-awareness kicks in. If I am doing the work, I'm developing myself. I'm working on myself. I'm just showing up in the world, walking in my purpose. What gives these other people the authority to tell me I must humble myself? I just honestly feel the words humble and humility are overused and misused. Many times it's misused in a way to deflect someone's own insecurities. It's just a reflection of whatever self-esteem issues they are going through because I believe being humble is personal. Humility is a stance that we, individually, have to sustain to continue to always gain the clarity and the revelations we need on our purpose-filled journey.

People have often misunderstood my confidence as arrogance. I believe arrogance and humility are both misused and misinterpreted. And when it comes down to it, it's all about perception and perception is a result of what life's mirror is reflecting back to us.

"We don't see things as they are. We see things as we are." —Anais Nin—

THE WIN

Confidence is connected to faith because once you decide and commit to pursuing the idea and the vision, the self-belief ignites from within, directly from your higher source. Self-belief upholds the trust within yourself to know what you are pursuing will work out. Every day you are going to get up and keep pushing because it's going to work. It has to work. Even though I can't see it, I'm confident it will work. Confidence allows you to reject the limiting beliefs, doubt, and fear of those around you. There's confidence in knowing it will work when somebody else says, *"Well, I don't know."* I'm confident because faith is the assurance that fuels my confidence.

I woke up one night with this thought and was smart enough to put it in my notes on my phone. So now that I have written down this idea, I will look through my resources and see how practical this idea is. If everything comes out how it needs to, I will follow through on the idea. I have faith in this idea and as I mentioned, faith is identical to confidence. I am not sure if this idea will work out in the long run, but I have faith that I will put all my might into it and try to make it work out as best as possible. My faith gives me the reassurance that this is something I can do.

I cannot express enough how crucial confidence is for achieving success. When you have confidence in yourself and your abilities, you are more willing to take risks, pursue opportunities, and persevere through challenges. And oh, will there be many challenges. You will need the motivation and determination confidence provides to keep trying and trying and trying when faced with setbacks or failure. The self-assurance allows you to transform your bold visions into realities. By surrounding yourself with the right networks, team, mentors, and supporters, you will feel empowered to believe and keep believing in yourself and act on your ambitions to reach for your dreams.

MINDSET CHECK

When people see my rise and comment on it, I say to them, *"If I can do it, you can do it."* With building The Mindset Snob brand, I recognize the need to talk more about my accomplishments publicly to inspire many others. I came from a humble background, transitioned from a 20-year career to opening a successful, seven-figure business within a four-year timeframe. I have talked at conferences about how to build a business, and I speak with youth about what it takes to be bold and confident in pursuing your dreams. You need to embrace and celebrate your successes more because others seek to be inspired by your transformation. Being that person where yes, I've done some amazing stuff, I also think about the number of people I was inspired by to accomplish my dreams of running a business, writing a book, and building a global brand.

Sometimes you meet amazing, bad-ass people, and then you learn their story and you're like, *"Man, why aren't you talking about this? This needs to be shared for the world."* I met a young lady one day and through casual conversation learned she did the branding for a major TV show. It was amazing to hear and so inspiring. I was like, *"God, why are you not talking about this more?"* Her response: *"Oh, I'm humble."* We must get out of this misinterpreted humble mode because people need to hear these stories. That person who is sitting in an environment that is not feeding them or it is not nurturing them will come across a story of a Bianca Wise or whoever sparks inspiration that's going to give them that last little bit of confidence they need to move on, transform, and start walking in their purpose.

Even as the author of this book. I had to realize it was time to come out and talk about my greatness. I need to be able to talk about my journey, my accomplishments; my story. Not in a cocky *"Look at me"* fashion but simply a desire to see everyone connected to me WIN by inspiring and empowering. Hopefully, others can take what they learn from me and go beyond their wildest dreams. If I keep all of that magic to myself, then it is not helping anyone. That is a little selfish, wouldn't you say? To win at everything you want out of life is about developing the flex muscle of confidence, which allows you to transform at every stage.

SNOB-VERB

"Confidence is the power to show up for yourself again and again. Confidence is the audacity to not be defined."

PILLAR 2

INDIVIDUALITY

"I win just by thinking differently than most."

THE STORY

Individualism is our existence in this world. It's our purpose and the reason for walking this earth in human form. Individuality is your highest point of creation, making us all unique. There's no right or wrong way to be a person, even though society will make you believe it. But when we walk proudly and embrace our individuality, we share our gifts with the world and the people called to be inspired by us.

I feel like my individuality is the reason for my unconventional trajectory in life, from working in the federal government, moving from that to the fire service, owning a fashion jewelry brand, and owning a home care organization. I've always taken a path that wasn't crowded and didn't follow after what everybody else was doing. I know that many people in the world don't want to conform to the masses, but they don't know how not to conform. My walk in this life is to show those people that you don't have to subscribe to the masses to be extremely successful, influential, and live an amazing life.

I think one of those unconventional aspects to my journey was that I did not graduate from college. When I show up in rooms, people always ask me, *"Well, are you in a sorority?"* and I'm like, *"Nah, I got my sorority. I'm a queen bee, see, that's where my sorority is, you know?"* Or people will say, *"What school did you go to? Was it an HBCU?"* People are often shocked when they hear my response that I am not a college graduate.

Let's be honest. What's the point of having a college degree if I can still be extremely successful in my 20-year career, starting and advancing a seven-figure business in four years, and showing up with the confidence that I belong in the room? I do not have kids and do not plan to have kids. For some, that is the biggest achievement in their life, but I am very firm in myself to know that I do not want children. My businesses are my babies, and watching them grow is the best thing for me.

If you look at my family history, I come from a group of people who were educators and worked in the federal government. A conventional pathway for me would have been finishing college then getting into education or working for the federal government. I tried the federal government path but did not like it, so I quit. That was the first time I quit a job. I worked for the FBI for three years during my early 20s.

I was working for the FBI when 9/11 happened. When I finally got home that night, something drew me to the recovery effort in New York. The work of the first responders was admirable to me. The first responders who put themselves on the frontlines to serve humanity drew me into wanting to do the same. So a month after 9/11, I resigned from the FBI. That started my pathway to emergency management. I took a job and a huge pay cut to work in an emergency room as a nursing assistant. It was a patient care tech position at a trauma center. I got so much excitement from helping people who were severely ill. No one in my family had worked in this field, so it was something completely new to me. However, with time and experience, I gained insight into what working as a medic and first responder in the fire department is like. That was the bridge that linked me to the fire department.

Nobody in my family has ever worked for the fire department either. As a young African American female, I knew of no historical figure who I could look to for motivation. It was just a thought, and I said, *"Well, this sounds like it's going to be fun, so let me try it."* Even today, you don't hear of or know of many Black women who work for the fire service. The number of Black women who promote up the ranks and reach retirement is minimal. The fire service is a white, male-dominated career. You wear a uniform every day, and you must stay conditioned mentally and physically to perform. But I could always add a little bit of myself to the uniform. At the end of the day, I am a woman, so I added my feminine touch to the uniform. Just because I worked with the guys didn't mean I had to look and smell like them as well, but do not misunderstand. I always got the job done.

THE LESSON

When you decide to operate and be your own person and think for yourself, you ascend and level up, moving toward whatever goal you set for yourself. Then once you have reached this ascension, the hardest lesson you will have to learn is that not everyone you know and care about will come with you, including friends and family.

Initially, it'll sting when you have that close friend you have known since elementary school and all of a sudden, as you are climbing the ranks, the friendship fades away and you are not close anymore. You don't even know why because in your mind, everything is the same and you are the same person you have always been. You start to realize that maybe soon after the friendship ends or later in life, the conversations change or somebody takes their path. You don't have similar interests anymore, so that relationship kind of fell off. That is the hardest lesson in understanding that your relationships will change as you keep moving forward.

You might have one or two people or family members who have just always been there and they're like, *"Well, she is who she is, so let her be who she be,"* but there are going to be relationships that just end.

During my fire department career, I had people I considered friends. As I moved into business ownership, we didn't have the same interests anymore, and I'm pretty sure I bored them with conversations about growing a business. Vice versa, they now bore me with conversations about things totally unrelated to my interests. Hence, it's not any animosity. It isn't that there was a beef or anything. It just starts to be this transition, and when you look back, you're like, *"Whoa, did I do anything wrong? Or did they do anything wrong?"* The reality is that it's just a different trajectory and pathway. You look up, and here come new people. So it's not always about friendships. It's about a network. People say it's lonely at the top, but I don't particularly agree. I believe it depends on your top because success looks different for everybody. Again, I feel like there are levels where you just attract other like-minded people for that period and they become a part of the network. Then as you keep going down your path, here come some more people, and here come some more people.

Owning who you are in its entirety can be difficult. Now that we are in this age of social media, we're comparing ourselves or self-image and our individuality to how others present themselves. And then there is the music that is conditioning our society to think about ourselves in adverse ways. The idea of what women are supposed to look like and what goes into modeling as it relates to surgery, style of hair, and overall curation of what the exterior looks like, which often is not real. We are all unique in our individuality. If everybody starts showing up looking like each other, then we don't operate within our full potential and our gifts disappear. The comparison leads to a lack of self-belief and confidence, which creates doubt and fear, making it difficult for you to transform into the greatest version of your purpose-filled self. Always remain confident, believe in yourself, limit distractions, and embrace individuality.

Social media is meant to be a tool. Like everything else in the world, you get back what you're putting out or what you're seeking. Whatever intention you have behind going on social media, that is what you're getting back. It's getting creepier and creepier to see how true that is. You could think about something and then go on social media and it's the first thing on your feed. I suggest limiting social media because it's media at the end of the day. Media is the biggest influence on social conditioning, mindset, and emotions. Curate your timeline based on things that will keep you inspired and keep you with a positive outlook. Follow people, places, and spaces where you aspire to be and limit all the other stuff that does not align with you. Do you know we can just unfollow, unfriend, and block people? It's very easy. Or how about this? Just turn it off.

One thing that I think is great that social media does is allow you to reflect upon your memories, good and bad. It's amazing for me personally to see my posts from nine years ago where I was talking about having a positive mindset. That makes me reflect and think, *"Man, I've been talking about mindset for a long time."* Those days when my imposter syndrome tries to creep in, I check in to reiterate to myself that, *"YES, I am a thought leader because for nine years I've been studying the power of mindset."* I have memories where I was talking about one day being a business owner, and then I look up, and I'm like, *"Damn, I did that."* So social media brings to the forefront good and bad memories. There are posts about old boyfriends and old friends, but guess what? I have the choice to reject the negative stuff and focus on all the positives.

THE WIN

My main dream in life has always been freedom. Meaning financial freedom, creative freedom, and freedom with how I spend my time. Initially, my thought process was that I was going to spend 25 to 30 years in my fire-service career. Since I would be so young at retirement, I would think about starting a business in my post-retirement life. In my opinion, entrepreneurship has always been the epitome of individuality. My desire to express my individuality became stronger, but it didn't quite fit the fire service structure. The older I got, the more I embraced my individuality. The conventional path was to think, *"OK, well, now I just need to conform to the fire department way of life and ride out the rest of these years. Maybe I'll get promoted to captain, but to get promoted to captain, I know I have to have a certain poise about me so I don't ruffle too many feathers or expose myself in a way that does not fit this culture here."* I thought about that. I thought, *"Let me just chill out, fly below the radar, not be seen or heard."* That would be the conventional path, but my fire department career got to a point where it just wouldn't let me grow as an individual, so I decided to leave. My initial plan of how and when I became a full-time business owner changed abruptly once I realized I no longer felt like I could thrive in that fire department environment.

Anybody who is spiritual or believes in God knows that you are dropped here on this earth in this physical form, however, you want to believe that there is a reason you were brought here. Many of us do not tap into it, while others recognize it. You're afraid to expose or fully walk authentically in it because of the herd mentality of society's standards. It's been said that we are God's highest form of creation, that is the purpose, and I believe a major part of our life is to live up to that standard. Purpose can change over time as you go through different stages in life. I believe there are permanent feeds where you are on a specific purpose, and then there are seasons or periods of purpose.

Walking in purpose is reciprocal energy because your purpose is gifting someone or others. Then at the same time, you're receiving the information, intelligence, and consciousness to keep improving and transforming. Some people feel as though their purpose is philanthropic. I have a purpose of serving humanity. That is a huge goal but you know, recognize that no matter how big your purpose appears to you, you could hold the possibility of immense positive impact. Your influence spreads and impacts another and then another, so it's just all magnetic. It's all connected. Understanding your purpose can help you focus on the greater goals. We are modular people, so the purpose is not just one particular thing we target. It shows up differently in different stages of life with different people for different periods. Still again, it's reciprocal, so as you're influencing someone else, you always are receiving feedback from the world on how to keep improving to transform.

MINDSET CHECK

Embracing your individuality becomes a part of life because individuality is our backbone as humans. We must ask ourselves if that thought we may be thinking regarding a particular topic is ours, or am I regurgitating it from somebody else? Do I want to agree with somebody because I don't want to rock the boat or go against the grain?

Do I want to follow the trends or set the trends? Individuality results in you thinking for yourself and thinking differently than most. When so many aren't secure in themselves, you can come across in ways that will trigger other people's insecurities. Or people will think you're crazy or unrealistic, especially when you talk about reaching goals and tapping into your power of manifestation. You start talking about the magic of being, doing, and having whatever you desire and applying the principles to get there. People will think you must be on some kind of drugs or alcohol or something because to them it's illogical and unrealistic. Key words: TO THEM.

For me, many beliefs I have now and have had over the years developed from my time at the fire department and paramilitary organizations. There's a hierarchy, and you have to follow direct orders. I would often be given orders that when I thought for myself, I realized did not make sense. The order may get someone hurt or could be done differently to result in something better. I was not given that flexibility for critical thinking or even offering up my perspective. So for that culture, I always came across as rebellious or unwilling to conform. In the fire service, everything is about being a brotherhood and a team, and the collective, group thought flows into it. Even if you know it is wrong, you just go ahead and go along with it. There's a book the fire department encourages you to read called the *Peacock and the Penguins*, and it's related to team building. The penguins do what they're supposed to do. Then this peacock comes in and kind of ruffles the strategies the group tries to put forth. I was always called a peacock, and I didn't take it personally. I think peacocks are beautiful.

In that environment, it was a negative connotation because the peacock is known to be the one that just won't conform. Even in personal relationships, a lot of times I think differently from friends and family. I am opinionated, so I will step up and talk if my voice needs to be heard for a specific reason. The people who love me already know I am bold and assertive, and actually find their own strength through my boldness. The people who don't particularly know me, don't care to know me, or have some type of secret animosity, generally shy away from me. There were instances in my career where I said to myself, *"Well, I'm a professional and I don't want to come across a certain way to my bosses or the public that I'm here to serve, so I'm going to fall back."* And doing so would kill me on the inside.

When it comes to my own self-improvement, I often second-guess myself but as I've grown older, I've learned the power of tapping into my confidence. I become more conscious of it, and that's when I tap into my confidence, which is just having that audacity to keep showing up for yourself. When I second-guess myself, I just stop for a second and tap into my self-belief and confidence. I'll ask myself, *"Is this the right move, or should I change something?"* But I never change the goal. You might have to change how you reach the goal, but the goal remains the goal. Now I don't want people to read this book and think that everything is just all peaches and cream and root beer floats. Everybody goes through challenges, processing negative emotions, discouragements and failures. The one thing that separates people who reach success is they know how to invoke the pillars that are discussed in this book. They also know embracing one's individuality can be a powerful driver for achieving success. When you are free to express your authentic self, you are more likely to pursue things that align with your passions, values, and natural strengths rather than conforming to others' expectations. Cultivation of your individuality makes you more resilient in the face of challenges because you are motivated by internal fulfillment rather than external validation. A distinctive perspective will always enable you to stand out from the competition. Trust me, I know! Individuality also fosters creativity and innovation. People who are confident in their own identity refuse to be intimidated by naysayers, doubters, or haters, and are bold in sharing their vision.

SNOB-VERB

"My mere existence brings in everything I need. I bring immaculate, genuine, magical energy into every room I enter."

PILLAR 3

VISION

"Logic will take you from A to B. Imagination will take you anywhere."

THE STORY

We all have a vision. It starts with imagination as children. We're born and gifted with imagination. It is actually one of our God-given gifts. When you're an adult, the context around imagination is that these things aren't realistic or these beliefs won't serve you whereas, for a child, it's a playful type of thing–something to keep you company or something that you kind of get caught up in if you're bored. The thing is that as children, society encourages us to imagine but as we grow up, we are stripped of that imaginative power. Leaving us to believe as we get older, we need to stay checked into reality. You stop dreaming, and imagination is just that; dreaming. When you're bored or idle with time, your mind will involuntarily flow into an imaginative state and we have to understand this is another sense, a higher faculty, gifted to us by GOD. Put some respect on it.

As adults, we get to a level where we can now put conscious effort behind what we daydream about. People who tell you to stop daydreaming don't completely understand how life works. The powerful thing about it is if you can dream it, you can conceive it. We have to be intentional about what we're visualizing because, with enough energy behind it, our daydreams will manifest. Many people are just unaware of how powerful imagination is. They know that they're daydreaming, but they're unconscious of the power behind it. One thing you'll consistently hear from successful people is: *"Don't quit daydreaming."* The visions that are being carried with you throughout the day are transforming you through the renewing your mind. You hear a lot about the power of having a vision and moving toward that vision but for some reason, many people just don't tap into it. I mean, even down to the music we listen to. I'm a hip hop, R&B person, and I know rappers are talking about vision damn near every song out there today or there's some type of relation to it.

We create the life that we want. Taking ownership and accountability for the negative situations and challenges that show up in our lives is difficult because it feels better personally to be the victim or feel victimized by other people. We want to blame others for the situation, but we created it all honestly. It's the universal law of attraction. The power of the mindset is exactly what Henry Ford said back in his day: *"If you think you can or if you think you can't, either way, you're right."* All control goes to our imaginary friend, the subconscious mind. The conscious mind is where our vision and dreams are held in the brain. The subconscious level of the mind does not know if what the conscious mind is thinking is real or imagined. You can visualize the most expensive, opulent place or thing you desire and your subconscious mind will believe it, connect into your higher source and start gathering what needs to be gathered to bring it to full fruition. This, my friends, is an unexplainable, magical fact. It's not until our vision transmutes to thoughts in our conscious mind that we apply logic, reasoning, and power to rationalize and disrupt our imaginary friend at work; the subconscious. The first thing we'll think is *"Well, that'll never happen."* The subconscious, backed up by emotion, believes whatever you tell it.

When we wake up in the morning, it's important that we set the intention of how we expect our day to go. It is easier to think of a negative thought than a positive thought. I haven't delved into the reasoning behind why it appears our minds gravitate to negativity easier than positivity, but one thing's for sure, we cannot shut off our thoughts. Since we have to think, why not consciously decide to think positively rather than negatively? That shift in the thought process will lead to *"Well, let me look at this subject differently"* or *"Let me not feed into the negativity."* When you adopt this shift in thinking over time you'll witness your results change. You may be faced with a difficult situation but come out of it feeling less stressed and confident to keep going.

I believe in the law of attraction which states we are always attracting what is likened to us. If you're idle or bored, why not sit around and think about good stuff like the ocean, taking a trip somewhere you've never been before, or spending time with family? Having all these images of things you love to do can rejuvenate and pamper you. If you do the opposite, it locks you into a poor attitude and stagnant energy that keeps spreading throughout your day. I often imagine where I see myself in six months. A specific goal where I get extremely detailed. Who am I with? What clothes am I wearing? What's the temperature like? I love to travel, I love self-care, and I love good dinners with awesome friends. Three months later, I'm sitting in an environment with great people and an amazing restaurant. I'm like, *"Is this deja vu, or is this exactly what I imagined several months before it really showed up?"* For many people, it's doom and gloom that takes over their thoughts. *"I'm gonna be broke for the rest of my life, and I hate this job, I hate where I live, I hate my car, and I hate everything."* Then six months down the road, nothing has changed and a sense of despair and failure keeps a person crippled. It is a very distinguishing result when you decide to imagine and have more positive visions than negative. Both are going to breed the results. You choose.

Being in the fire department was costing me my imagination. Your home and work environments are big factors as it relates to your emotional health. The toxic environment of my work was killing me softly. Energy is contagious and when you're in a toxic environment for long hours where most of the people you're surrounded by are not happy deep down, realistically, many people are not happy. They're not happy professionally. They're not happy personally. The happiness some people display is often a facade, unfortunately. Then you add in the nature of my particular career, where you're only showing up during a crisis or disaster. As a first responder, you rarely have experiences where it's a joyful, happy ending. Usually, instead, you are witnessing someone die or their house burn down with all of their stuff?

I got into a space where I went into defense mode to try to protect–or have the feeling I was trying to protect–the little sanity I had so that when I ran home to retreat, I could get away from it more profoundly. But by the time I got home, I would be so exhausted. I just wanted to go to sleep and then wake up the next day and do it again. In that environment, it became mind over matter for me. I desired to be surrounded by people of like minds; the dreamers, the visionaries, but that's also relative because, in that type of career, the like minds I was surrounded by were just people who worked for the fire department. Some who were like me, losing their imaginative power. All we talked about was fire department stuff, emergencies, and disasters. There's rarely an opportunity to talk about professional or personal development. If you are the one who initiates the conversation, you are looked at like a stranger because nobody wants to talk about "that stuff." They want to talk about disasters and emergencies, and it became extremely exhausting.

It reached the point where I made a conscious decision that it was time for me to remove myself from the environment. I would feel mentally and emotionally exhausted to the point where I would take a lot of time off from work, and my coworkers would laugh at me. But it was honestly necessary for me to check back into the reality I was creating where there wasn't turmoil, bureaucracy, unhappiness, and craziness. That's how my first business B. Foxy Jewelry & Accessories developed. That was my creative, imaginary outlet. It allowed me to tap into my creativity when I wasn't at work and find joy in accessories and jewelry and everything that can be done with it.

THE LESSON

I knew of 1st responders who worked for fire departments for 30 & 40 years. I never could see myself saying in a celebratory way that I stayed at a job for 30 years, not even the 25-year mark I had to hit for my initial plan to take root. That wasn't even reasonable to me. I initially thought I would make it to 25 years, but the negativity of the environment and some of the people surrounding me was too much. I would see one chief officer frequently, and I would greet him by: *"Hey chief, how are you doing?"* He always said, *"I'm living the dream,"* and I'd be like, *"Whose dream is this?"* This was not my dream. One day I asked: *"Chief, honestly, is this your dream? Like, is it really?"* He explained that it was always his passion and goal to become a firefighter, and he was proud of how he rose through the ranks. And I felt that honestly was the dream FOR HIM. While thinking to myself: *"That's not my dream. This is just a job for me."* But the problem is when you speak differently or speak against a collective mindset as such, you are labeled differently. That's why I saw my dream as something I needed to protect day-to-day.

Your vision is the easiest thing to protect because only you see it. If you want to get it out, you can journal about it. Journaling is the best practice of getting the dream out of your head for several reasons: 1. when you write it down, it starts to take form. 2. it still remains your little secret. Even if you want to share your vision with people be careful, most won't understand it. Rightfully so, because the vision is only for you, not everybody else. Not your friends, not your family, not your coworkers. So the easiest way to protect it is to not talk about it until you find that tribe of people or that mastermind who understands because they are of like minds. They also have curiosity, exploration, and success. You protect your vision at all costs through conscious decision-making. Remove yourself from the environments that no longer serve you. Find an outlet, and finally, do not talk about the vision unless it's with people who understand and fully support you. Also, ask yourself are you on a trajectory to transform and transcend yourself for the better? That isn't going to be with your friends or your family nine times out of 10.

THE WIN

Our self-image is linked to our vision of how we see ourselves, and I don't mean our reflection in a mirror. I mean in your mind. How do you see yourself? If you're content with it, OK, fine. But if you're a person who wants to be better, do better, have better, there's a renewing that you have to go through.

Pretty much everyone's learning new things and unlearning things that no longer serve them. There are habits that you need to develop and a belief system that you need to replace or modify. Ask for guidance because you can't do it alone. We as a society spend a lot of time getting permission, asking permission, and wanting validation and approval from people who either don't like themselves or don't even know themselves. Connect to your source to seek guidance. Form a spiritual practice, ensuring that you are tapping into that. You must do the work. You have to work on yourself.

We sometimes tend to want to play the victim or not hold ourselves accountable for what's showing up in our lives, but 100% you have to take ownership of that. We have to get down in the trenches and "do the dirty work" independently. Your vision can be killed when you're not taking ownership as it relates to you. You'll never be able to develop. People always like to say, *There's levels to this*, which is correct. Every next level in life requires a new level in your mindset and as a person, so learn to take ownership of things, and understand what you need to do to improve yourself or change things. Again, what do you need to learn? What do you need to unlearn? Often people just go through life with less favorable characteristics, and they'll say, *"Oh well, that's just how I am."* Wow, really? Do you feel as though that's just who you are? Like there's no better way, or there's no other option? Or do you not want to take the time and do that work to change some things to get to that next level? As a victim and not taking ownership, you're not able to recognize the things that no longer serve you or the hindrances or blocks holding you back from showing up as your best self.

MINDSET CHECK

I am the actual physical manifestation of this entire book because I can speak confidently on everything being discussed. I did it and still do it, and the results show up. Many people will ask me something like *"Well, how did you grow your business so fast?"* I'll sit and think, *"OK, which answer am I going to give them?"* They're looking for strategies, tactics, and organizational or business plans. I have these things, but I move forward with my beliefs in the power of my mindset. I had a vision of being a successful business owner with multiple businesses generating a lot of income, inspiring a lot of people and serving society at the highest level. But what type of person do I have to become to do that? I had to stop spending time on distractors like watching a lot of TV, and limiting social media, to start finding new networks, and new thought processes. I have to read, and I have to develop myself. All of this I'm speaking in this book has resulted in me being where I am today.

When I was little, my mother used to say that I was the most nonchalant child she ever had, and that would get me in trouble because apparently to her I lacked emotion. In reality, I express my emotions differently from what others expect. But I was also that child, teenager, and young adult who questioned the status quo. I always want to know: *"Who made these rules? What are their credentials, and what makes them the expert?"* I always carried that boldness. When you are the one that's questioning the status quo or the norm, you're automatically misunderstood because most people don't have the confidence to step up and speak out. When you are that person, your words can be perceived wrongly. My intention was never to be difficult or disrespectful, I honestly had a valid question, and I feel as though because nobody has the answer other than some regurgitated, *"Well, that's how it's always been,"* or *"You can't question that,"* then you're perceived as a troublemaker. If it doesn't sound right to me, I will ask the question.

That did get me in trouble a lot in the fire department. I was always being charged with insubordination because I was asking a question that they deemed I should not be asking. You build up all this data through the years that, as a child, you don't even really know what you're doing. Then when you become an adult you realize, *"I've been collecting data all my life."* Honestly, a lot of the stuff that we're living up to, there is no real reason behind it other than somebody's recycled beliefs passed down through generations. Why do I have to subscribe to it? I remember something that my mother said a long time ago: *"You observe what everybody is doing in the room, and then you do the opposite."* That makes sense to me because what will happen if I don't conform? Are they going to kill me? I don't think the result will be that bad. Especially when you're being led by an unwavering vision that you're destined for greatness.

Readers should remember to never quit daydreaming. Think of the highest, grandest, craziest, unrealistic dream that you can dream for yourself and be relentless in your pursuit of it. Don't allow anybody to tell you not to or that it's wasting time because that's not true. Dream, show up for yourself everyday, do the work, keep the faith, then watch the magic happen.

SNOB-VERB

"Dream that shit. Then real life that shit."

PILLAR 4

GRATITUDE

"If the only prayer you said was 'Thank you,' that would be enough."

THE STORY

Growing up, I joked and said I was an only child. I felt that way because my brother was seven years older than me. So by the time I was in my adolescence, he was pretty much grown and by the time I hit pre-teen, he was a grown man. So I was always a child who, during that influential time, was close to my mother and auntie. For some reason, I have always gravitated to older women. To think back on my early years and growing up in a Black household, attending black church, etc. there were certain things we just had to do and expressing gratitude for just about everything was one. We had to say our prayers at night, say grace before every meal, and went church every Sunday and be grateful to be able to spend another day in the house of the Lord. Religion as it relates to the expression of gratitude was a non negotiable in my family. Going into my career as a first responder, I experienced traumatic and destructive crises like fires and other unfortunate events. During the holiday season it would always sadden me to respond to a call where someone's house was completely burnt down during Christmas time.

All the gifts and the house were gone. Sometimes multiple families would be affected and they would lose everything. A lot of times the Red Cross would be the only resource to support people with their basic needs following an event like that.

As a first responder, you often dread the period between Thanksgiving and the new year. The expectation always is it's the time of year for crazy shit, and there are a few valid reasons as to why. The holiday season creates a hectic scene in our society because people shop and some work extra hard to pay for gifts. Studies show that heart attacks and strokes rise this time of year because people are in the go-go mentality through the new year. Also, homes are at a greater risk for fires because people fry turkeys at Thanksgiving and they don't particularly fry them safely, which triggers many house fires. In addition, families start to put up Christmas trees adorned with beautiful lights and gifts but will forgo proper care of the tree, specifically the live ones.

One particular story that stands out to me is when a fire started in a townhome community during the week of Christmas and spread to multiple homes overnight. A grandmother was upstairs and bedbound. She suffered third-degree burns over 90% of her body and had to be rescued from the house. I was the paramedic there to handle the medical aspects of the rescue. The house was completely engulfed in flames. The grandmother was the worst, but two children also had injuries. Because the structures were all attached, it spread to three houses. Hence, approximately 20 people were displaced. The grandmother succumbed to her injuries. She was elderly and on oxygen, and third-degree burns are significant. Skin is completely burned to the level of charring. That was a situation around the holiday where I went home feeling so grateful for my life, my home, my family, friends, and my belongings.

I recall another medical call two days after Christmas, which was significant because it created a law in Maryland for distracted driving. A family was on their way to the mall to return a gift when they were rear-ended by a pickup truck. The impact killed a young boy who was a backseat passenger. His name was Jake, and his family fought to get Jake's Law passed in Maryland after the crash because the driver that caused the accident did not face any criminal charges. The entire incident was unfortunate because the driver who rear ended the family was on their way to work. They were texting, got distracted, and hit the back of the vehicle. They got no jail time, and I don't think they paid any fines. That is why the family pushed to get the law passed. Under Jake's law any type of vehicular manslaughter that occurs when the driver is texting or being distracted on the phone is $5,000 and a year in prison. That day, I was the first to arrive on the scene. It's a traumatic experience arriving and watching a father doing CPR on his son in the middle of the interstate. Again, you go home and replay these thoughts in your mind about how that has an adverse effect on so many people. With all the empathy I had for these families I had a greater sense of gratitude, being so appreciative for my safety, the safety of my family, making it through the day, and getting from point A to point B."

At one point I did ask myself: *Is it a selfish thought that I am appreciative that I still have my home to return to?* Realistically, it's not selfish. It's just reassurance that it does not matter the hardships, challenges, frustrations, or whatever you waddle in for that day. You might think it's the worst day in the world, but then you come across someone who has lost their entire home right around the holiday or a medical call where a father goes into cardiac arrest on Christmas Eve while his daughter is home from college.. You think about what that memory will be for that family every Christmas. Those moments were significant reality checks for me. Regardless of how I may have felt after being cut off in traffic, being pissed off by a boyfriend, or coming up short for a monthly bill, before I went too far down the rabbit hole of negative emotions, I grounded myself back into gratitude. I come across an emergency like that, and it will always snatch me back into my reality and have me saying, *"Well, that is a little hard, but I have my health. I have shelter, and I am safe. I am grateful.*

THE LESSON

For me, when it comes to gratitude, it runs deeper than a *"Thank you"* to someone. It became a conscious act to sit and immerse myself in the feeling of gratitude. That is the one thing that makes me want to keep getting up and going because I sit and process what I am grateful for instead of just saying, *"I am grateful for my friends and family."* Sitting, absorbing, and processing what it all means is an elevation of the mindset. It's been an elevation for me as an individual, an adult, and honestly, through my career. The purpose of my job was to always show up during crises, destruction, and death. For so many years, I experienced extremely tragic and traumatic situations and was in chaos and crises. It was grounding and a release for me to come back focused and centered with the understanding that this time we have here on earth is extremely precious and gifted to us from a higher source. Our job as people is to ensure we are enjoying this journey in full abundance and appreciating every detail along the way.

Our society has grown to where so many are constantly seeking instant gratification. People believe something is supposed to be handed to them or the world owes them something, forgetting to be grateful for the simple pleasures like to wake up in the morning, having shelter, having all your bodily functions work without assistance, having food, and not just feeling loved and appreciated but also showing love and appreciation to others. Those little things are powerful but as a society, we are reaching for the big stuff and not being grateful for the little things that support us daily. If people checked into appreciating the little things more, maybe there wouldn't be so much depression. How can you be sad when you sit back and process the positive and magical things happening in and around you? That is not to discount clinical depression, which is so very prevalent. But I believe if some people take time to focus back on their surroundings and how far they have come, it might reset their emotional scale to come out of sadness and start appreciating their life more.

THE WIN

When I speak of focus, it is a key factor required for transformation and elevation, getting to your win, and becoming successful. You also have to focus on improving your self-image to become the person you aspire to be. With focus on yourself, you need to constantly develop different and better habits that will keep you grounded on the journey to elevation, success, or your win. I believe grounding yourself in gratitude is key to keeping you focused. At least for me, it reels me back in when I do start down a path with beliefs and thoughts that do not serve me for what I am aspiring to be. It's what I consider a ritual. I don't know if ritual and habit are the same, but it is all about developing yourself to a point where your higher self always leads you. That is not to say the lowest self does not challenge the highest self. Still, you can get to a point where your higher self is where you are present the most, and that requires energy. I am a firm believer in energy. I do not know how people do not believe in energetic responses from us as individuals, but energy is contagious. It is proven that the most practical and easiest way to elevate your positive mindset and positive energy is through gratitude. If you want to show up as your higher self, you must develop a gratitude ritual that practiced over time will involuntarily just take you there.

Gratitude is that one emotion that immediately takes you to a higher vibration. Whether you believe or not–some people believe, some people don't–we all are here vibrating on different frequencies. Our energy connects to our emotions through a scale that goes from most negative to most positive. To sum it up in basic terms, the negative end of the scale includes: anger, frustration, jealousy, envy, and competitiveness. All of that lower vibrational shit. You've seen the memes shared on social media saying, *"I am vibing high,"* but I don't think many people know what that actually means and what is required. To say that I am only interested in experiencing high vibrations starts within yourself. The expectation is not for the next person to vibe high or have high vibrations for you to feed off of. It's all you, you set the tone. Then the magic of the source–God, whatever you want to call it–attracts the likeness to you. The likeness of other people, places, and things that are forcing this feeling of love, joy, and comfort–all those higher emotions like happiness, elation, feeling tranquil, content, and grateful. Believing and understanding there is an emotional scale set inside of every human that acts as a compass for us on this life's journey. When we choose to stay on the positive end of the emotional scale, life just becomes so magical and abundant even when the bad shit shows up. I have matured to a point where it is now my belief that the negative thoughts are fraud and do not serve me, so I will not dwell on them.

MINDSET CHECK

The connection between cultivating gratitude and developing a winning mindset is strong because gratitude breeds optimism and positivity. Focusing more on what we appreciate allows us to see the good around us and feel uplifted, which in turn provides a hopeful perspective that fuels motivation and self-belief. It also helps us see abundance rather than lack. If it's one sure thing that will hinder success, it is scarcity thinking, each and every time. But thankfulness reminds us of the resources, relationships, tools and talents we can utilize to achieve goals. In addition, all winners will need to tap into their resilience from time to time. When challenges arise, and boy will they arise, gratitude helps us cope with setbacks and bounce back quicker, and to persist through difficulties on our path to success.

If you have a big ego, gratitude will certainly put that ass in check. The way it combats entitlement and overconfidence is actually quite funny. Sometimes success can go to your head and ultimately set you on a path you didn't believe you signed up for. Gratitude will show up at the perfect time to knock the sense back into you. Appreciating all we've been given keeps us focused, humble, and hungry, which in turn propels us to higher levels of achievement. I have been witness over and over again to how a consistent practice of appreciating the good nourishes my mind, body and relationships. When the inner strength meets up with all of the outward collaboration, it puts you in a prime position to fulfill your potential and feel unstoppable.

Train your mind to recognize the countless gifts we've been given, daily. I suggest keeping a gratitude journal where you record at least 5 things you're grateful for each day. Implement it as part of your morning routine and watch the magic start to happen.

SNOB-VERB

"Gratitude is so gangsta."

PILLAR 5

SOLITUDE

*"Do not be afraid to disappear for a while to
see what comes to you in silence."*

THE STORY

In 2012, I ended up getting sick. Initially, the doctors did not know
what was wrong with me. I spent nine days in the hospital, and in
hindsight, I knew exactly what was wrong with me. I was stressed out
from the environment at my work because that was the year I was
promoted to lieutenant. Once I got the promotion, it seemed like the
feeling of being overwhelmed and stressed from the years of disparity
and bigotry just went to the next level. For months, I was showing up
in this energy of being defensive. Every day, I was getting in trouble or
always being called into the office for allegations that always seemed to
result in being unfounded. I had so much built up tension, an unhealthy
level of it. I would be preparing to start the shift thinking, *"What are
they going to do today?"* or *"What's going to happen today?"* and one day,
my nervous system went "OK, enough!" That brought me to a 9 day
hospital stay. Doctors didn't know what was wrong with me. I went
through a battery of tests from every specialist you can think of and

finally, they diagnosed me with an autoimmune disorder, ulcerative colitis (UC). In reality, I didn't realize how sick I truly was until I was finally discharged. My entire gastrointestinal tract suffered a severe level of inflammation. I returned home in a weakened state and I had a three-month recovery ahead of me. I was sick to the point where I had to have a home health nurse come in every day to change bandages from my wounds from my body's secondary, atypical response to the UC. Coming from a small family and having a small circle of friends, my support was limited during my recovery. If I asked for help, people would come to my aid, but I didn't want to be too much of a burden. You can't expect people to step out of their careers and their children and other obligations to be by your side, so my three-month recovery became a period of solitude for me.

As the weeks progressed, I got better, and my home health nurse reduced her time with me from 5 days to three days a week. The dermatitis that developed from the UC created so much pain. Sometimes the wounds were so painful I couldn't sleep. In my opinion, solitude can aid in all healing whether emotional or physical because it opens a portal to self reflection. I thought, *"OK, I am too young to be ill like this. Nobody in my family has an autoimmune condition like this. Where is this coming from?"* I became more aware of my health and what I needed to do to avoid getting so stressed about things that I can't control; especially when it reaches the level that makes me ill. I came to realize I had nothing to prove to my coworkers or supervisors. I'd been employed there for nine years and had a stellar employee record. I'd made it to the rank of lieutenant, and was the first Black woman in the 180 year history at the time to do so. Why do I need to keep showing up trying to prove myself? So for the next 2 1/2 months, I decided to focus on myself. I focused on improving myself through my mind, body, and soul. The start of my transformation to my highest, grandest self by improving my mindset.

I was released back to full duty at work after a couple of months, and my team of doctors were so surprised because they expected me to take at least one year to fully recover. They did not expect me to heal in the timeframe I did. I was like, *What?* My illness was significant to the point that my gastroenterologist had my case published in a medical journal because my autoimmune condition was very atypical. They were shocked when they saw me back to 95% when I went for my final follow-up. He wrote my final prescription and added a little note that said: *"Happy holidays, Congratulations."*

THE LESSON

Solitude is your level up. Solitude, by the general definition, is being alone but to me, it does not mean being lonely. People tend to confuse being alone with being lonely. In my opinion, they are two different sides of the coin. There is seclusion and just that act of unplugging from people, devices, places, and environments, all of that being quiet detachment. So being lonely is putting you in a space where discomfort exists. Solitude is not in a spirit of loneliness and should not bring discomfort as it allows you to become your #1 accountability partner.

Feeling lonely tends to lead to the need of having to be with someone or having to be somewhere, or having to do things all the time, even if it's things or people you don't particularly like, aren't particularly good for you, or aren't serving you. However, you still attach yourself to them because it feels better than being alone. It is a place that will foster discomfort because even though you are surrounded by things and people, you're damn sure not happy. When you intentionally work towards gaining more self-awareness, solitude becomes more and more comfortable. Our society has become so locked in with "stuff." Media, and the need of being in the know, being part of the crowd, being with people, being on the scene, being in the club, or being at the happy hour. You need to know that's not healthy replenishment that supports your overall wellbeing. For me, replenishment comes from retreating to my solitude, which leads me to more opportunities for self-reflection, recalibrating my focus, and gaining clarity on things. Solitude also sets our thinking mind in motion and helps us harness the power of positive and creative thinking.

What society is dealing with in the present day is the inability to like your own company. Going into solitude helps to align and connect to your inner being and start to uncover your authenticity, and soul's purpose. When you start to spend that intentional time with yourself, the layers start to peel back. You start to learn yourself; like really learn yourself. Sitting with yourself, your thoughts, your shit can be uncomfortable. But it puts you on a pathway of *"How do I improve this or what do you need to do to improve?"* When you get to a place of liking your own company and loving yourself unconditionally, that makes you a whole person and brings you into alignment with your purpose. You start to show up in the world differently; healed, not broken. Never in search of outside validation from people. You do not need to be validated by people, things, or places.

Solitude also gives you the ability to ground yourself and even comes into play to heighten your spiritual practice. Limiting the distractions around you to ground yourself and connect to your source becomes powerful moments you never want to forgo. When you can slow down and get comfortable with yourself, it boosts your confidence, elevates your self-belief, raises your standard, and helps you self-sustain. You walk differently and talk differently. There's no need to conform or feel like you need to be a part of a crowd or know how others think. You can think for yourself, and you'll recognize how you think differently than most, shifting your perception of the world, having clarity, tapping more into your intuition, and even a more robust imagination. I believe that when we are placed on this earth, we have everything we need inside of us to enjoy life and live abundantly. Still again, this GOD given power gets so muted and overlooked because of all the distractions we deal with all day, every day–whether it's your commute, your children, your spouse, your vices, or TV media. Going into solitude allows you to detach from all that noise and tap into your inner power where everything you need is right in front of you. Through that comes clarity about questions or an impasse you may be at if you are unsure which way to take, or being indecisive about things that could move you further in life. Direction for all of that comes from within, but you have to know how to limit your distractions again so it becomes clearer to you. That's done through solitude.

The other positive thing about solitude is having a front seat view of your growth. In my opinion, the most badass thing you can do is observe your personal growth, which comes from improving habits, belief systems, and overall transforming your mindset. All of that is done through the clarity you gain in solitude. Even how it influences our relationships, especially our romantic ones. There are so many "situationships" going on nowadays. Many people are just seeking surface level traits and characteristics in others they believe will make them feel better or validate them somewhat. It all goes back to what people are seeking outside of themselves. One thing we always hear is *"he or she completes me,"*--that should not happen as nobody else can complete you. It should be two whole people coming together and partnering together in this thing called life to create a great life experience. Other than that, if you're looking for somebody to make you happy or give you a nice lifestyle, you will always be seeking and will never be satisfied. You're not going to be completely content and happy with that dynamic. As you get to be comfortable in solitude, you learn what you will and won't tolerate and your value, self-worth, and standards. I think society has put a negative connotation on the thought of solitude. Again, it has nothing to do with being lonely. As a matter of fact, it's quite magical.

THE WIN

As adults, we all deal with limiting beliefs to a certain extent, no matter how successful we become. Doubt will always creep in, but as you become more aware and powerful with your mindset, you reject it as soon as you recognize it. You learn how to immediately reject those thoughts and redirect to a more positive thought process. Through my personal growth, I've witnessed how I've become better at shifting my thoughts as soon as a doubt will try to show up. I'll put on my favorite music, or listen to a video that is uplifting and motivational to recalibrate and get back focused. Also in my journey, I've learned that I would much rather be happy than be right. We tend to waste so much time wanting to debate people, and go back and forth trying to change the minds of others. I've gotten to a point where I am like, *"You are right."* They could be wrong as 2 left feet, but hey, they won! In my younger days I would find myself in situations where I probably could have gone hours going back and forth with people, and now I'm just like, *"Yeah, no, you got that one."* Having the ability to be in a place like that is a blessing and is something that I would not be able to do if I did not spend sufficient time with myself to understand that I have nothing to prove to anyone.

MINDSET CHECK

This social media world we live in results in a gross amount of comparison that curates and highlights unrealistic perceptions of how life should be lived. Everybody is a millionaire and everybody is grinding, everyone is living elevated lifestyles. But when do you rest, recharge, reset, and sleep? Personally, leading a seven-figure organization does not allow me to keep up with the trends and personas of the social media image. Half the time, I look straight crazy in the day to day of being a CEO, but being able to show up in real life, off screen in my authentic self creates an amazing level of freedom, but I'll digress from that soapbox.

Practicing solitude has shown me that even my relationships are reflections and that was a hard lesson. Spiritual law says the people in our lives reflect us. So you usually get agitated or frustrated with other people because you see those behaviors or traits in yourself. This is why I'm very selective and intentional with relationships now. And at this big age, we all should know that every relationship does not equate to friendship.

In society, we use the word friendship loosely. We can all be sociable and amicable and not necessarily be friends. We can be tribal and not necessarily be friends. Now being very conscious about people, I'm able to recognize when I don't like something about someone, instead of dismissing them or pushing them aside, I take a step back and dig my nail into myself to say, *"OK, what is this insecurity or what it about me that is making me have this sense of this person? It's something that they are reflecting in me."* But also, let's keep it real. Sometimes it's just low vibrational energy that my spirit will immediately reject. That has been huge in my dating life and relationship with me. Before I got married, I would gravitate to guys who weren't good for me. After a while when I recognized certain patterns of behaviors, instead of getting mad because of how he's acting, I started to take a step back and figure out what I am seeking or feel I'm lacking that is creating this affinity for him. Is it daddy issues? Is it loneliness? Is it just boredom? That's supreme personal growth when you become more conscious of yourself with your interactions of others. The dynamics of your relationships start to change. I feel like now I can learn something from everybody I meet. I don't care who you are. It might be me learning what not to do, what not to say, or how not to behave. Still, whatever it is, I can learn something and reciprocate because we all align with each other for a purpose. With my relationships, I'm at a point in life where I can't be taking too much from you, and you can't be taking too much from me. We have to have some type of flow, balance, and reciprocity with all of this. I should be able to help you, you should be able to help me, and we should respect each other's boundaries.

Solitude is as important as the breath you breathe. Solitude is your level up, and it's also your power. It is where your power lives and waits to be tapped into. Solitude is satisfaction. Just satisfaction with life. It helps with your creativity, productivity, learning, and overall contentment, happiness, and satisfaction with your life path. It's intimacy with yourself. Falling in love with yourself over and over again. Liking and loving your whole self, flaws and all.

SNOB-VERB

"Minding my damn business eliminates half the problems in my life."

PILLAR 6

FOCUS

"Focus on what you care about. Everything else is a distraction."

THE STORY

Focus is the energy you feed your desires to bring your dreams to life. What that entails is not just limiting distractions but rejecting people, places, and things that do not align with the end goal you have set for yourself. Who created this lie that we can multitask and spread our attention far and wide and still be successful? There's a Roman proverb that says *"A man who chases two rabbits catches none."* In my opinion, focus will always need to be applied differently depending on the end goal. Let's say you have a deadline that you have to meet for your job that requires blocking time and censoring your attention around specific tasks that you can accomplish to make sure you're able to complete the project or at least get it to the next step. That's a task-driven focus. Then there's this overall focus as you're moving along your journey and you're visualizing that person you want to become or that self-image you aspire to obtain. It is important to focus on all those positive attributes and environments because that will help you develop, grow, and reach the next level. So again, it's rejecting everything else that does not align with that end goal.

Right now, my most important focus is my personal and professional development and my self-image. The one thing that I have learned is that we cannot outperform our self-image, and our self-image draws in everything we are seeking in life. Self-image is the gateway to manifestation. When going through life and trying to achieve something, you always need to hold the image of the person you want to become and what that looks like. When you look at me, I am a leader, meaning I choose to always show up to inspire, guide, and connect people every day. I have a team of more than 50 employees who look to me to have all the answers, even though I don't. Still, I need to always show up and be ready to figure it out. So I am focused on developing and educating myself, which goes hand-in-hand with my other goal to build a world-class business. I want to build a company with a reputation that precedes itself. I want people to know that we are truly taking care of our clients and that we are a business they can trust with their needs. The last thing you want to hear when working in the healthcare service industry is that your service is of poor quality.

Now we transition into my personal health journey. It is no secret that I am a proud member of the 40-plus club. After my health scare in 2012, taking care of myself has been a priority for me, but now it's with a new emphasis. Before I was just an employee who had to be in good shape because that was required of me in the fire service. Now as I age and am in the role of an employer hiring and overseeing people, I need to ensure I prioritize my health and wellness by eating well, having a healthy self care routine, and getting the right amount of sleep to remain on top of my game.

Having been a business owner for quite some time, it's evident that the ongoing journey requires an unwavering focus on both personal and professional growth. It's easy to utter those words, but when you realize that despite all your experience, you haven't yet reached the level you aspire to in these areas, it can be a somewhat fearful realization. Especially when you step into a room and must put on the cloak of leadership for those who look up to you, a sense of imposter syndrome can creep in. You start to question yourself, "Should I truly be leading these individuals, or would they be better served by someone else?" Some might dismiss imposter syndrome, but for me, it's a near, daily challenge.

To the point where, even when I look at my achievements, backed by accolades, I still ask myself, "Did I really accomplish that?" That nagging voice in the back of your mind feeds you negativity, making you doubt your worthiness of it all. Escaping this mindset is no easy feat. What I've discovered is that you must remain acutely aware, for if you let your guard down, that second guessing will find its way in. You must swiftly reject all those foolish thoughts before they start to fester in your mind.

Affirmation becomes crucial. Remind yourself that, yes, you achieved those things, that, yes, you built this business, yes you are a bad-ass. This kind of mindset doesn't come effortlessly. Even I, to this day, grapple with it. While others perceive me as a confident woman who has successful businesses and exudes self-assuredness, the reality is that I, too, question myself just like everyone else. The journey to overcome this involves maintaining a positive self-image that aligns with your own vision of yourself.

THE LESSON

Energy flows where your attention goes, so if you have a goal, you must put work behind it. You just don't wake up and say, *"Oh, I want to make $1,000,000 this year,"* and then it drops into your lap. There has to be work, energy, intention, and nurturing behind each desire. You have to reach a point where you're clear and concise about the goal. If you're completely distracted, you may still reach your goal, but being distracted and worrying about stuff that does not serve you at that point or does not serve what you need to be doing to get to the goal slows you down. Focus on the things that serve you, that will create the momentum needed to bring your goals to life. I think that might be the easiest definition of focus: All people, places, and things that serve you and your highest good need to be put at the forefront of your attention because there's a lot of stuff out there that ain't serving. It might be funny at the time or catch your attention for a moment, but then you have to check back in with yourself and say, *"Well, what does daddy's new* *baby mama got to do with me and trying to get to this degree?" "Why am I arguing with a stranger on a social media platform about a celebrity lifestyle that has nothing to do with me?"* You look up, and it's two hours later. You've wasted two hours of your day arguing with somebody you don't know over something that has nothing to do with you.

THE WIN

Consider this idea that, *"Focusing on the people, places, and things that serve you for your highest good will always yield positive results."* Believe in it and implement that daily, and you'll get into a space where you want to see more positive results, and you understand that the pathway to getting those positive results is to stay focused on the people, places, and things that serve you.

Something that I constantly say and subscribe to is I mind my damn business. If I had to define personally what focus is, this would be my definition: *"Just mind your damn business."* When you do so, you limit distractions as much as you can because we're living in a world where distractions are almost impossible to escape. I suggest implementing certain boundaries, and time management techniques like applying a time limit to your social media use, browsing the internet, or watching TV. Setting and standing firm on your nightly bedtime. Also, putting your phone on Do Not Disturb for a period of time to get important tasks completed. Applying one or all of these techniques consistently over time will yield positive results and when that one result shows up, you're like, *"Oh man, I did that."* It gives you more confidence about the next time you're going after something. It becomes harder not to subscribe to this mentality so every day, you wake up and affirm to yourself *"I'm going to mind my damn business today and make it a great day!"* You have set your day up on the right course. Focus leads to consistency, and consistency matters much more than perfection.

Adopting and applying a positive mindset as much as possible is how I've gotten to the point that I am at. It's one of those things that is hard to explain with words, but if you wake up every day determined to lead with good energy, positivity, visualize what you want and stay focused, then it's hard to imagine how you cannot achieve the goals you have established.

When I wake up every day, I embrace my individuality and step into my power. That means that I intend to think for myself, to know and love the fact that I was given a mind and a brain, the ability and the power to tap into my thought process and think for myself. I understand that as an individual, it is God-given power and I don't take it for granted. Own your results. If you're not getting the desired results, there's nobody else to blame. We often blame it on everything. *"Well, that show on Netflix was so good I couldn't turn it off."* How did you allow a TV show to take over your time? You could have easily picked up a remote and cut it off. Now because you allowed this distraction to take you away from your focus of the day, you failed to do the laundry, cook dinner, or prepare for your presentation tomorrow and it's completely your fault.

MINDSET CHECK

We as humans can be extremely complex in day-to-day life. We have multiple obligations. You may be an employee, a parent, a spouse, and a student. You need to be present within those roles to get through the day successfully, so I don't believe in a set, defined work-life balance. People always talk about work-life balance. In my opinion, striving to achieve a work-life balance is unreasonable. What has to happen with us as adults and people who are always seeking to achieve more is to find the appropriate balance for that particular day. Let's say you are an aspiring author and must focus on completing that chapter or your foreword. It just so happens that on that same day, your child needs their braces tightened or somebody has the flu. This is where the skill of prioritizing comes in. It is OK for you to decrease the amount of time or not even touch your chapter to ensure that you're focusing on getting the children where they need to be.

If you're a scholar and you're going for a Ph.D., that dissertation may need to be done by the end of the week. Still, you also have some extracurricular activities or maybe a side hustle where you have to deliver on something. You may have to say to yourself, *"OK, hold on. I know my dissertation is due on Friday, and I know I promised a customer I would get their product by Friday."* Sit down with yourself and hone in on what can or should be prioritized. I feel as humans sometimes we're just too hard and rigid on ourselves. That we should subscribe more to a "life flows like water" mentality. Every day we just kind of go with the flow of it all. If you try to be too hyper-specific about how much time you'll spend here or there every day, you're going to end up crazy. Or you're just going to exhaust yourself mentally and emotionally trying to chase a perfect work-life balance that does not exist. The great thing about focus is it's 100% controlled by you. Focus also connects to your confidence. Show up confidently every day as the individual who chooses to be selective and very intentional about where their life is headed.

Remember, focus is the light that guides us through the darkness of doubt and distraction, and ultimately leads us to our full potential.

SNOB-VERB

"Life is so much simpler when I drink my water and mind my damn business."

PILLAR 7

FAITH

*"You have to undoubtedly believe no matter what cards
you are dealt, you're going to be successful."*

THE STORY

Faith is simple. You either have it or you don't. It means once you decide what you want to be, do, or have in life, no matter how big the goal appears to be or how discouraging the statistics are, you will achieve it. Faith, for me, is complete confidence and trust in my higher source that my desires will unfold in perfect timing and perfect design. So often when we don't see the physical evidence of our prayers, we'll get frustrated or discouraged because it's not showing up how and when we think it should. In my prayers, I always ask for the divine design, meaning that I want it to manifest with the magnitude only God can perfectly align. When you are specific and surrender the details of your goal, it shows up the way it's supposed to show up for you. Trust me when I tell you, you have to remain confident in the knowing that the end goal is unfolding.

When I started my fire department career, young and eager, I believed that I would spend a minimum of 25 to 30 years in that field because that's what you're conditioned to believe when you join the fire department, police department, or federal government. You work half of your life until you reach retirement age and then you live out the rest of your life on a fixed income. Many people in these fields work past retirement age because they can't truly afford to retire. I subscribed to the idea for the first 8 or 9 years. My mentality was that I had this nice comfy job, they paid me a nice salary, and in 25 years, I was going to retire. Then they'll send me a retirement check every month and that will be setting me up for the rest of my life. I also thought that I would climb the ranks to reach an executive officer level, again having the same mentality that *"If I make it to the rank of chief by the time I retire my pension check will sustain me for a modest life. Then after my career, I'll become a diversity, equity, and inclusion consultant and go around to help fire departments develop a solid DEI plan."* For a portion of my career I was so focused on creating how life would look after that fire department. In hindsight it's clear that I was adopting the goals and visions of those I was surrounded by.

Then in 2012, I launched my first business venture, a side hustle called B. Foxy fashion jewelry. It was a bold, edgy, and unique collection of fashion jewelry and accessories. It became very popular amongst my family, friends, and a few influencers as well. I enjoyed it so much that I started working extremely hard towards developing an actual brand. I started taking classes in professional development, brand development, business development, how to start a business, how to grow a business, and how to exit a business. After gathering all of this business-related knowledge, I started shifting my focus a little bit. I fell in love with the idea of having my own. My mindset took its first shift with me now believing that I would retire after 25 years and then live out the rest of my days as a full-time business owner. Through the years, I continued developing myself for business ownership and overall leadership because I loved everything business-related. I continued to network and attend events. I would find myself in rooms with successful people making $1,000,000 a month or $100 million a year in revenue. They just seemed so free, and they had nice lifestyles, and they're running businesses being badasses. They're buying businesses and taking advantage of investment opportunities. So my mindset took another shift, and I thought, *"If somebody can make $1,000,000 a month, why am I choosing to remain in an environment where I don't feel valued and I'm not operating at my full potential for $100,000 a year?"* What started out as a hobby and something fun to do because I wanted B. Foxy to be more than just a side hustle developed into dreams and visions of not making it to 25 years at the fire department. Talk about a WTF moment. When the desire of full time business ownership started showing up consistently, my mind would reject it immediately. Just the thought alone of leaving my good government job gave me chills. Then as time went on, I became more miserable, dissatisfied, and stressed with my work environment. The thought of me promoting beyond lieutenant made me nauseous, and at least once a month, I found myself going back and forth with peers who either made significantly less than me or outranked me, and definitely weren't as creative or ambitious as me. That was the nudge that shifted my entire trajectory. I no longer subscribed to the idea that I was going to complete a 25-year career, retire, be healthy and thriving, receive a pension, and be young enough that I could move on to start another career. No, that did not work for me anymore. So to quote the great Shawn Carter (Jay Z) I took a leap of faith and let my eagle wings spread, spread, spread.

THE LESSON

Faith has to be plugged into a higher power at all times. That has nothing to do with organized religion. The real blessing is spiritually knowing that something greater and more powerful than you always supports, guides, and directs you. Having conviction and believing without a doubt that everything is always working out for your greatest good. This is real faith.

Some people may look at that and say, *"What about the negative things that happen to us?"* People need to realize that things are not happening to us, they are happening for us. We need to learn from these experiences to redirect ourselves. Having faith in your higher source should bring comfort to your surrendering under the undesired circumstances. The human part of us will find difficulty in letting go and letting GOD. But the resistance will continue to build until you decide to choose faith and dump all doubt and fear. Faith is the driving force in helping you achieve anything you want to achieve. It will bring optimism and resilience, to help propel you through obstacles and challenges. Let's be clear; there will be challenges. Become comfortable with welcoming challenges when they show up. Challenges are good for our growth and transformation. The magical part about faith is it helps you recognize that success comes not just from your own efforts but from gifts beyond yourself - be they spiritual or community support. Though the path may be arduous at times, unwavering belief in yourself and your purpose fuels the passion and drive to keep moving forward on the journey to success.

THE WIN

Walking in fear is a result of having a lack of self belief, confidence, being disconnected from your source, seeking validation from outside sources and indecisiveness. It's the opposite of your greatness and it minimizes your GOD given power. It takes away the ability to provide the gift that you're put here to offer the world. So please tell fear to go to hell.

All of us are placed here to share and contribute something to the world. Fear and doubt don't allow you to walk in your purpose. It doesn't allow you to be inspirational for those seeking out people like you. When I say I'm fearless, that doesn't mean that I don't have fear. It just means that I fear less so I feel the fear, and I push past it. I don't let it cripple me or take me off the path. That has always been a strength of mine, in my opinion. I don't care if my voice shakes, if I'm sweating, or if I'm about to throw up. I'm going to be bold, take action, and push forward.

Will Smith once said during an interview, *"What is on the other side of fear, you'll never know."* Yeah it may be a failure or what people perceive as a failure, but what if it is everything you ever imagined or better? Allow your faith to guide you as you follow the road that is unfolding for you. Know that you are placed here for a purpose and the creator created you to bring greatness to life and gave you the power to do it in many different forms. Above all, putting your faith into action by following your convictions with confidence, despite not knowing the outcome, will build your big faith flex.

MINDSET CHECK

There are several ways you can develop your faith muscle. The one I subscribe to most is you must surround yourself with like-minded people most of the time. Energy is contagious. If you are on a path to excellence and greatness and hang around a flock of toxic folks, then you're going to become a part of that negativity. The saying goes, *"If you hang around four broke people, you're going to be the fifth."* "Misery loves company" is the truest cliche. Ask yourself: what environments am I putting myself into and what type of relationships do I have close to me? Are you surrounding yourself with people who are smarter and more talented than you? They are the ones who are going to help you expand your vision and hold you accountable to that vision. The people, places, and things you immerse yourself in have to be mainly positive. They must have mindsets of success, abundance, prosperity, love, and happiness. Your environment will have a major influence on keeping you inspired or sad, encouraged or mad. Choose wisely.

If you don't subscribe to anything else in this book, subscribe to this. Faith goes against everything logical. That's why it's so often said that you have to have "crazy faith." Without genuine belief in the impossible, yes I said impossible, the manifestation of your dreams rings hollow. Ultimately, faith gives us the courage to detach from specific outcomes and align ourselves with divine wisdom and timing.

SNOB-VERB

"Trust in the process. Even when it seems it's not processing."

PILLAR 8

RESILIENCE

"Sometimes you wish it were easier. But if it were, everyone else would be doing it. Then you remember you don't want to be like everyone else."

THE STORY

Resilience is often the backbone that leads all of the highest-performing people we know to the success they have garnered. It's the main ingredient of success. If you do not have resilience, you will give up on your journey at the first site of any resistance.

Part of my understanding of resiliency was learned from my mother. My mother was very strong. She never complained about anything, even when she was super sick. I only saw my mother get upset one time throughout her whole illness. I think we as women, especially Black women, take on this invisible made-up story that we have to be superwomen and we always have to be strong. I don't know where this comes from, but that's a different topic for another book. It's like for some reason, Black women have to claim this badge of honor of being so strong and unwavering. A lot of times that does more harm than good. Now as I'm older, what I recall from my childhood is that I had a single mother, and she had no choice but to be a superwoman. She had to keep going for her two children to make sure that as children, we didn't want for anything. To this day, I don't know how my mother did it. I found one of her pay stubs some years ago and I was shocked because I could not understand how she survived raising two children as a single parent on that type of money. But to her children, we were alright. I didn't believe we were poor because it didn't feel like it to me and she had a good job working for the federal government, so I couldn't see how that was possible. I knew we weren't rich either. Regardless though, my mother never allowed us to make excuses. She would ask, *"Why didn't you clean your room?" "Oh well, my stomach was hurting." "OK, well, what does the stomach have to do with your room being dirty?"* She never allowed for too much justification. If you're going to do something, that's your word and you're going to do it because your word means everything. If you're incapable of doing it or unable to follow through, speak up and say something. Or don't commit to it. Best-selling author Don Miguel Ruiz discusses in his book *The Four Agreements* that one important principle in life is to be impeccable with your word.

So this is all to say my mom was a hard worker. There were days, especially as she was starting to get more ill and I could see that she wasn't feeling good, but she would take that ride to D.C. from Baltimore and be at work for eight hours and then make that commute back from D.C. and do it all over the next day. She never complained or asked for time off. She just knew that was her job and she needed to be there to do it no matter what, especially knowing that no one would come to save her or her children. She needed to do what she needed to do to provide for us.

People are always talking about how hard things are. For instance, if somebody says they're interested in starting a business, usually the first response they'll hear is how hard starting a business is going to be, usually from someone who never started their own. If I am speaking honestly, I've never had anything come easy in my life. I always tell people you have to choose your hard and take action to do hard better. By choosing your hard, you have to remain resilient especially when the hard you chose is really rocky. You will get knocked down constantly and resilience is you just getting right back up and dusting yourself off. This age of social media makes stuff seem so easy. Everybody is a millionaire overnight and everybody's making all this money. In reality, that is just not the case. The law of gestation works equally for everyone and states that every seed you plant has to go through a period of development before it's actualized. Just like a baby. During the gestation period, a lot of things will show up to distract you or especially discourage you, but you just have to get up and keep going.

For my entire fire department career, I had to be resilient. Not just because of the type of work I was responsible for, but also because I was a Black female who was not born into a family of people in the industry. It was all new to me. Still, with the training I had to go through to become a firefighter and paramedic, I would have days where I just wanted to throw in the towel. But I got up the next day, and I pushed through that resistance. When I was hired into the fire department, I had already obtained my paramedic certification, but I was kept from operating at the paramedic level. They held me back for about nine months because they kept telling me my skills weren't strong enough. Out of the 40 people in my fire recruit class, seven had their paramedic level certification. I was number seven, the only Black female, so I was going to be labeled as the one that's not strong, not competent, and not skillful enough. The thing is, the best paramedics are those who come from being great EMTs. Nine months of functioning at the lower level of EMT was just setting me up for epic dopeness. I didn't cry about it, I just decided that I would become the best EMT the department had ever seen.

When I hit that nine-month mark, one of my white male colleagues who I consistently worked with could not understand why I was being held back. He was so upset that he decided to talk to my superiors and tell them they needed to allow me to start functioning because I was a very strong provider. He wrote a letter to my battalion chief, lieutenant, and captain telling them he had worked with me consistently over several months. He said the department was doing themselves a disservice by not allowing me to function, so I ended up rising to the paramedic level shortly after that.

Fast forward nine years, and I was the third person out of the class of 40 promoted. I was the second one of that paramedic group of seven to be promoted, so I surpassed all but one of them. But you see if I had gone along with that discouragement about not being a strong provider, if I had allowed that to keep me down or plant some type of limitation in my head, my trajectory to becoming the first Black woman promoted to lieutenant probably would have been different.

Another story of resiliency is just me taking the leap into full-time business ownership and how all of that has unfolded. I left the fire department and went to open my in-home-care agency while I had B Foxy operating on the side. The first challenge I met when trying to start my in-home care agency was my licensing process. Operating a business like mine in the state of Maryland requires what is called a residential service agency license. Initially, I was not told that the state of Maryland had a 12-to-18-month approval time for this license. Imagine you just walked away from your job to start a brand new business. The first challenge you're hit with is that you may be facing a year to a year-and-a-half before you can even get licensed to operate. That was not an option for me because I absolutely was not waiting that long. I couldn't wait that long. Ain't no way I'm waiting that long. So with my resiliency, I had to figure out a plan because I was not just going to sit around and wait for somebody else to tell me when I could start serving my community through the valuable services I was ready to provide. I kept reaching out to the licensing department office to the point where I probably became a nuisance. There was one lady who pretty much oversaw the office, and this lady was so mean, but I mean rightfully so. She was inundated with calls from people like me constantly asking the same questions. Still, I would just call and be the friendly voice she heard. In addition to that, I decided that I would go to Annapolis, the capital of Maryland, and meet with my delegate to see if they had any hand in getting my application pushed forward. Again, I was not going to wait 12-to-18 months, so I was showing up there every two weeks. I went to the delegate's office, and her chief of staff was there because the Legislatures were always in session. The chief of staff was the only one available to talk. I talked to him every two weeks. I would go down there, and he would be like, *"I gave her the message. I talked to her about it. We don't have anything else that we can do."* In my friendly voice, I would reply, *"OK, well I'll see you in two weeks,"* and so then I would be back in two weeks. I did that about four or five times, and luck swung in my favor one day. Through perfect alignment, I received a call from the licensing office much earlier than I was initially told. To put things in perspective, here's the timeline of events: I applied in January 2019 and that second week of February was when I received the notification that it was going to be about 12-to-18 months to process the application. February, March, and half of April I spent going back and forth to my delegate's office and as I said, she was not there. Still, each time I would drop in with the Chief of Staff and say, *"Hey, how are you doing?" "I'm just checking in."* And then the second week of May, I got a phone call from the office that does the licenses with the surveyor stating *"We have your application on our desk, and we're about to start the process for approval."*

Fast forward to November 2019. I became licensed and fully open and operational. That was about 11 months total for the process versus the 12-to-18-month timeframe they said it would be before anybody even picked up the phone to talk to me, so that was resilience. Then six months later, a global pandemic hit. Geesh.

THE LESSON

There are five ways to become more resilient. One is to TAKE ACTION toward your vision. Ideas without actions don't become goals, they become regrets. The others are to develop a spiritual practice, adapt to holding yourself accountable for everything you do, and know when to rest. But one that I don't think gets enough attention is your mindset. You have to check your mindset more than you check your phone. Always end the day with self-reflection and affirm you did your best and that when you wake up tomorrow, you're going to try again. Also check in with your thoughts. What are these thoughts that I'm having? Are they serving me? If they are negative thoughts, you need to reject them immediately and replace them with better thoughts. All of us have a responsibility, and we have to take accountability to stop and check our mindset and make sure that we are always moving forward with intentions to think more positively and make sure our thoughts and beliefs are serving us for the better. That's why it's extremely important to surround yourself with like-minded people who have been through what you are going through. Frequently you will need to ask for help or guidance or have a vent session with others who will help you in various ways.

Because I am writing this book, you may assume I have all of this mastered. There are still some days when like any other human, negative emotions filter in. Still, every time I experience discouragement, it becomes easier and easier for me to be resilient by rejecting any thoughts that don't serve my highest good and refocusing back to positivity. I may be going through a tough time, feeling discouraged and the universe will reveal to me in a subtle, comforting way that it's only temporary and to standby and wait for the lesson. It has taught me everything that I subscribe to and discuss in this book: to just believe in myself and to stay firm in knowing that I have all the tools I need to push through. To this day GOD is still teaching me that I need to be more patient with myself because the first person I'm pissed off at is me. This truth has taught me to step back and relax a little bit and not judge myself too hard because judgment clouds focus. When you are in a situation where you need to redirect or pivot, you need as much clarity as possible. I have learned to laugh at myself and not be so serious with some things. It has taught me the importance of having a spiritual grounding because it is the set point by which you can pray, meditate, and be open to the answers you receive from your source. It's good to have your circle of people you can vent and complain to because sometimes you need to do just that. But also be mindful to limit those sessions as you are just strengthening that negative energy that keeps pulling you back into uncertainty. A spiritual grounding, remaining in faith and gratitude, and just trying to make sure that when you go to sleep at night you're not holding onto too much of the past is critically important so that whatever happened today gets cast away because I know when I wake up in the morning, it's a new day.

THE WIN

Growing up in the inner-city of Baltimore, the narrative most times is to become a statistic. Then being born to my mother, a teen mom who had two children by age 23, is another strike. We didn't have relationships with our dads. That's another strike. We grew up in a complex neighborhood of Baltimore City. There goes another strike. We went without a lot of supervision because we were from that latchkey kid era, so when we got out of school, mom wasn't home from work yet. We had to let ourselves into the house. We had to police ourselves at an early age, and we could have easily been caught up in craziness just because there weren't too many people to watch over us.

Baltimore City has a quirky culture of pride in the neighborhoods you grew up in, and we will always battle over which is better: the east side or the west side. It's like two different worlds, even though it only takes about 20 minutes to travel to the east side and vice versa. It's like traveling through a different state. I grew up on the west side of Baltimore but went to high school on the east side. Just that travel from where I lived to my high school was all kinds of stuff that I could have been sucked into that would have led me down a different path. Again coming from this strong Black mama, I would probably have much rather gotten hit by a car than have to deal with her parenting style and reaction if I were to call her from jail or have to tell her I had gotten into some type of trouble. I probably would have just run away first. But I think any child who has grown up in an inner-city with so much crime and drugs and hopelessness every day requires resiliency. To be able to say you've never had to go to jail, never got addicted to drugs and alcohol, maintained your mental health, did not have any illegitimate kids, and are not in the system is, unfortunately, not the norm.

There's a story back to when my mother passed away. I blamed myself for that for a long time because of my career in healthcare and being a paramedic. My mom ended up moving in with me the last two weeks before she died . I remember I was working an overnight shift in the fire department, so I was leaving one night to go to work and I could tell she wasn't feeling good. I kept asking her *"You want me to take you to the hospital?"* She was like, *"No, no, no. I'm fine. Just go to work."* I worked in the community I lived in so my fire station was right around the corner from my house. That night about 2 o'clock in the morning, we got a call in my neighborhood. Riding past the back of my house, I could see that the lights in my home were still on. I thought to myself, *"That's kind of weird"* because mom would go to bed early and if she wasn't sleeping, she would like to read a book. She wouldn't have the lights on, but I didn't think anything more of it. We got canceled from the call, so I didn't have to do anything regarding it. I didn't have my house keys with me, so I was like, *"Well if she's sleeping, I don't want to ring the bell."* It was 2 o'clock in the morning and I didn't want to disturb her, so I just went back to the station. When I got off the next morning at 7 a.m, I went home and found her unconscious in my basement. She had been there overnight, which is why the lights had been on all night. So I had to call the ambulance and they transported her to the hospital. She was extremely sick and septic and passed away the next day. It's like you have these thoughts of, *"I'm a medic out here saving everybody's life or making a good attempt at it, and then when it came to my mother, I saw where it was somewhat of a decline. Still, I ignored it because she said that she was OK, although intuitively, I knew she wasn't."* I had always blamed myself for not pushing her more, and I went to therapy around it. Grieving the loss of your mother never really goes away, you just learn how to cope with it. But early on, it opened me up to a sense of failure. I felt I wasn't there as best as I could have been for my mother, the way I was for strangers. I know that I absolutely cannot have that type of burden on myself and that everything happens for a reason. Those last two weeks that she moved in with me was an amazing time shared. I just feel like that was the path that was supposed to be taken.

I am extremely blessed that I had a mother who, throughout her life, had so much resilience and fought for everything to provide for her family. She taught me and raised me into the woman I am today. Even though she is gone, the essence of her and her guidance and example remains.

MINDSET CHECK

The importance of remaining resilient is that it is how we get to our wins and it is how we learn about ourselves and become wise on our journeys. It has to be a part of our journey because as I said before, never expect anything to be easy. Do hard better. Some things may appear less challenging than others but for the most part, most things worth having are just not going to be easy. I say that because the way we picture it in our minds, it never happens that way. It's extremely important to remain resilient because it helps you to understand when the path starts to unfold in a way you didn't imagine, it does not mean that the goal changes. The goal remains the goal. How you get to the goal might have to change. You may get knocked down seven times but you better get up eight.

With spiritual practice, you get to a point in life where you realize anything that you imagined or anything that you envisioned you can have. You can repeat mantras and affirmations like *"I can do anything."* That is true, but for things to manifest, we have to flex our muscles and take action to go along with the journey and surrender and follow how the path will unfold. It may not go the way you expected it to, but you have to relax, keep the faith, keep the gratitude, show up, and try the next day again until you get to that point when you look back and are like, *"I'm living what I once prayed for."*

Be patient! I want to reiterate, we cannot control the timing of anything–again, it's the law of gestation. As long as you wake up and you still feel passionate and you still feel grateful and joyful and have clarity, just keep pushing through. When you get to those points of frustration, anger, haste, losing focus, and all that negative stuff, then it's time to just chill out and allow yourself to be led by your higher source in order to receive direction on what your next step should be. We should rest every day anyway because that is how our mind and brain recharge to become clear and allow the answers we seek to show up. You might be resting one day and the answer to a question you've had just pops into your head and you become renewed to pick back up and keep trucking.

SNOB-VERB

"What the fuck do I look like giving up when today might be the day I win."

PILLAR 9

HABITS

"Habits can decide the course of your life. Take the time to build a solid foundation through your habits, and your life will forever change."

THE STORY

Our habits should be ever-evolving and always considered because habits are how we show up in the world. Most of the time, habits are led by subconscious activity that we do not realize we are doing. Habits are consistent behaviors created through habitual thoughts and beliefs. As we want to elevate in life, it is going to require changing our perception and outdated belief systems around things. Literally, it's a massive shift in our thoughts, feelings, and behaviors which is partly done through developing new habits.

Our habits are what drive 95% of our day and our productivity, whether positive or negative. It comes to a point where we need to adjust the whole belief around why we need to continue or stop a particular habit mainly as a result of our conditioning and beliefs. Habits are changed in one of two ways. One is through a repetitiveness of action over and over, which is often difficult because of a need to develop discipline. The second is an emotional impact. Something that feels like a slap across the face or like you've hit a brick wall—a wake-up call.

One popular topic that relates to our habits is our diet and nutrition. In 2012, I hit a brick wall. I experienced an emotional hurdle that required me to change my eating habits overnight. I went from being able to eat all the cakes and cookies that I loved to literally having to eliminate every morsel of food that contains wheat, barley, or rye in its ingredients overnight. In the western diet, that's pretty much everything delicious. A gluten sensitivity took away my ability to be comforted by all my favorite vices; a piece of cake or cookie on demand. When you do drastic lifestyle changes like that, it's a major shift in your paradigm and leveling up of your mindset and consciousness. Now in order to maintain my health, I have to restrict certain foods, and I have no choice. It's not a choice or preference, it's life sustaining. If I eat food with gluten containing ingredients, I become ill. My body rejects it and rejects it severely. The abrupt adjustments I had to make is high up on my list of the hardest shit I've had to go through, but I am surviving without it and my health has markedly improved since I was diagnosed with UC. The question becomes, what was subconsciously placed inside of me before having the gluten sensitivity where I felt I always needed certain types of foods that now will make me sick? Was it comfort? Control? Satisfaction? I don't know. Going out to dinner, the expectation is to have cake for dessert. Now at a new level where I can't have it, it is easy for me to not think about cake or cookies. The question for me specifically is what was prohibiting me from just going away from that habit without an introduction of a health condition that forces me not to have it.

As you elevate in life and you want to improve living conditions, a lot of times your current habits or things you have been conditioned to believe, such as lessons from family members or the conditioning from how you were raised, can hold you back. Habits are important because they quantify improvement, success, and reaching goals. They always have to be reflected on to assess whether or not a habit still serves its purpose for the goal or the level you are trying to reach and to have the courage, will, and effort to push when it's difficult to step out of that comfort zone. Usually, changing a habit requires one little tweak or being more conscious of behaviors to stop and replace with improved behavior.

Society and your surroundings also plays a huge role in our habit-forming. I will say the experience of spending nine days extremely ill in the hospital, being poked and probed, having tests run, all to find out I need to stop eating grains is something I absolutely don't need to go through again. They told me I would have to take multiple medications to keep this autoimmune disease in check, and I did not want to accept that as part of my new way of life. I was in my early 30s at the time, and I did not want to have to take lifelong maintenance drugs. So the question became, is my desire for sweets worth the risk? The frustration sometimes comes from being around family and friends who either do not know what gluten is or are misguided and don't know how to react or accommodate. Eventually, though, that also works itself out with education and open communication.

The challenge became very personal for me. How do I go from being someone who enjoys great food and all types of cuisines to someone who has to watch what they eat with regard to gluten? It was already a built-in habit. The only way I was going to change was to develop new habits. This meant overhauling my refrigerator and pantry to throw out the food I could no longer eat, researching ways to modify my favorite dishes, and just eliminating certain things altogether. I needed to change cold turkey. I needed to look at my life and decide how I was going to fundamentally change so I no longer was driven by the urge to eat foods that were known to make me ill. It also came down to building a new routine. Instead of waking up, walking into the kitchen, and eating the first cookie that came into my eyesight, I had to instead look for something else. Now you may not know what it's like to have a raging sweet tooth, but it is torture to want a warm chocolate chip cookie and instead have to replace that desire with a chocolate rice cake. Lawd, this was not life but eventually, my ability to select better choices became automatic; my habits changed.

According to James Clear, Author of the best selling book, Atomic Habits, it takes anywhere from 18 to 254 days to develop a new habit.

I changed my mindset and started to think differently around how and what I should eat in order to remain feeling and looking good. I developed rituals, routines, and practices that helped keep me focused on developing my new diet, and of course, you can see I am doing swell. But when developing new habits you absolutely have to develop discipline and remain motivated. You need a routine, practice, and accountability to keep going in the right direction, or else you will get the same unwanted results over and over again.

THE LESSON

While in the fire department, I created a morning ritual to help me get through the day. It consisted of waking up much earlier than required. I never was the type to sleep half the day away but creating a habit to wake up extra early did require discipline. I would get up early to give myself time to slow down and set the intention for my day. My morning routine consists of when I wake up, the very first thing I do is express gratitude. In addition to being thankful for waking up, it is intentional gratitude. I am grateful that my bones are waking up with me. I will wake up and bask in how the sheets feel. The warmth of winter or the coolness of summer. I lean off the bed, wiggle my toes, and express gratitude to my body for being functional. The process of going to the bathroom and going through the first-morning pee. Thank you, kidneys, for functioning. It might sound silly, but it is powerful. Once I get all of that out, I journal for 10 minutes. The journaling changes each day. One day it may be journaling about goals, or it may be writing my thoughts. However they show up, I'll just write them down. Sometimes I journal my disgust for something, or how somebody had ****** me off. I'll write about that. I just get stuff out, whatever it is at that moment, and then I meditate for 20 minutes. After I meditate, that's generally when I start my workout routine which is usually no more than 30 minutes. On weekends, it can run longer, maybe an hour to 90 minutes. Then I start my day.

My morning routine also includes not checking social media or looking at e-mails. I don't check text messages. I don't check missed calls.

60

I don't turn on the news. I don't turn on the TV. If I turn on anything, it might be a YouTube video of Wayne Dyer, Earl Nightingale, Joe Dispenza, or Abraham Hicks–all the teachers who talk about elevated consciousness, and mind science.

Another habit I have created is time blocking because time moves faster than we want it to. Still, honestly, the one thing that's equitable across the board for everybody is the amount of time we get every day and every week. It is our responsibility to ensure that we are utilizing the time we are given everyday productively. Being productive means focusing on what needs to be done to move toward the goal. As it pertains to my businesses, it's imperative I time block and focus strictly on the important tasks first. Everyday at noon, I know I need to pause whatever I may be doing and take a break to eat because I have developed the habit of intermittent fasting also, and my eating window for most days is between noon and 8pm. I am not always consistent, but that is what I strive for. I mean, let's be honest, we're all distracted by our surroundings and external forces, and as much as you plan, prepare, or time-block there are some days where distractions will continuously pop up, but for the most part, set the intention to remain focused on the task at hand as much as possible.

As hard as I work, I am not a subscriber to this current culture and society of *"Hustle till you die."* I'm on the grind 24/7. When I decided to take on business ownership full time, everybody was like, *"Oh, it takes up so much time. You will have late nights."* Yes that is true, but what was and still is true for me is, I'm taking my Black ass to sleep on time every night. News flash: sleep is very important. After all, for most of my adult life, I spent two nights every six days working a 14-hour shift overnight in the fire department. The firehouse is set up as a house with living and sleeping quarters. You have beds to rest when you're not responding to emergencies. More often than not, that bell is going off all night long, so you don't really get sleep. Even if you get the downtime, you don't get that appropriate deep sleep that is required because you're in an energy of anticipation, waiting for the next run.

Everybody wants to talk about the hustle and the grind, but nobody wants to talk about that spiritual level of the purpose of sleep. Hustle and grind exhausts you. It takes all of your energy and the purpose of sleep is a reset, recharge, and rejuvenation of the mind, body, and soul. Often, that's when the answers will show up or the downloads will come. Our subconscious mind needs that state of rest to help us align our dreams and give us the clarity and direction we are seeking.

I'm 40 plus at the time of writing this book, and when people find out my age they will often be surprised and compliment me. I always relate it to my habits of getting proper rest and staying hydrated. I literally drink water and mind my damn business. So many illnesses, poor attitudes, aggression, and feelings of frustration we encounter from others throughout the day can be fixed by sleep and hydration. So most nights, unless I have to attend a late event, which does not happen often I am in the B.E.D. at a reasonable time like 9 p.m.and asleep no later than 10:30 p.m. Now on a good night, especially the time of year when it gets dark early, I might be in bed at 7:30 p.m. and sleep by 9 p.m., but I'm getting at least eight hours of rest, sometimes 10. Sleep is BAE.

THE WIN

Habits are our key to success or failure. Think about this for a second. When you look at Mark Zuckerberg, there was a big deal made years ago when he discussed how he basically wears the same outfit every day so he can focus more on his business than wasting his brain power or seconds of his day on what he is going to wear. He and so many other successful people have developed great habits and routines that they follow rigorously and that have allowed them to focus on the goal achieving and productive actions that gets them to their wins. This needs to be the way you approach your life. You need to build habits and routines that best allow you to maximize your output and stay engaged with what you are trying to accomplish. Here's the wonderful thing about this; it is entirely in your hands. You know what you can and cannot handle. I told you a little about my morning routine. That may not be something that you subscribe to, but you have the ability to build it the way that suits you. We all have the ability to be successful. I don't care what anyone tries to tell you. There are God given superpowers in all of us that allows us to be, do, and have every good thing we want in life, but it does not happen by accident. It happens by us taking the appropriate steps and keeping a positive mindset to propel us to the riches and successes we are trying to achieve by being disciplined and intentional with your thoughts, feelings, and behaviors.

Look at your current life and think about what you can change in order to maximize your daily output while also getting the necessary things into your life. You need good sleep, good nutrition, some daily activity to get you moving, and simply a great attitude. Try to build these into your routine, but then try to add things like meditation, affirmation, and journaling first thing in the morning. Do things that resonate with you like listening to music, reading, or studying personal development material. Stick to them, get the work done, and watch as your life begins to transform in front of your eyes. Remember anyone can be successful but you first need to put in the work to make it become your reality.

MINDSET CHECK

If I can take a moment here to self reflect, in the past I have not been the best active listener. I had the habit of cultivating a response before the person even finished their thought resulting in me not hearing or comprehending what they've said. We could be having a great conversation, but in my head, I am developing a response. Because I would be so locked in on my response that I'm about to give you, I wouldn't completely hear what you said.

The best example I have of this is with regard to my relationship with my husband. His way of thinking is the polar opposite of how I think. Now to create context around this: I'm an Aries, a fire sign. It's said that we're impulsive, but we can multitask, and in many instances we move faster than we probably should and we don't think things through often. In contrast my husband is a Pisces, the total opposite. He will think and rethink and rethink again. I have made 35 decisions before he even makes his first. When he talks, he paints the details of every part of the story. My brain does not necessarily want details. I need the point. We can be 17 minutes into the conversation, and I'm thinking please get to the point. When my brain realizes he's going into details, active listening goes off, and I will completely check out awaiting the point of the story. I realized through the years that I absolutely could do better and he deserved better than me constructing an answer that didn't align with his question because I had no clue what the hell he just said. So I decided to do better and develop a better habit with active listening. When communicating with my husband I have accepted that he is detail oriented. I eliminate all distractions by putting the phone down, I come away from the laptop, and focus so I can listen to what he's saying. Then when we finally get to the end of the topic, I have feedback or a suggestion. I don't know if that's an Aries thing or if that's just a bad habit, either way now that I know better, I do better.

Thanks to him, I developed the habit of active listening to people even when they go into a 20-minute monologue when all I needed was the last 3 minutes. I am not perfect, but I am learning to improve, which is what developing good habits are all about. You learn over time, and you often learn where you can improve in your life. Watching yourself grow will be your favorite series.

SNOB-VERB

"Outgrowing yourself constantly is a vibe."

PILLAR 10

MINDSET

"May your mindset shift the whole damn universe."

THE STORY

Our mindset is built on the collection of our belief systems, thoughts, perceptions, and attitude, all of which provide the direction of where we are going in life and how we will get there.

There is no right or wrong mindset. Your life will deliver to you whatever mindset you subscribe to, positive or negative. I believe mindset is our god-given superpower. No one can take it away from you, but the world and society highly influences it. If you allow it, the world can control it. Adults do a bad job of allowing their external situation to dictate their mindset. We give over control to others too easily. I say your mindset is your superpower because you can adjust it when needed. If you are not yielding the results you want out of life, you can trace that back to your thoughts, beliefs, attitude and actions and change each of them at any time. Your habits are within your mindset because they create the actions you take in life based on your mindset. That is the beauty of it all: Whenever you feel like you are not heading in the direction of success or unfavorable events keep showing up, you can trace it back to how you are thinking or not thinking and change it instantly.

I check my mindset constantly, especially now as I become more conscious because it is so easy to gravitate toward thoughts and beliefs that don't serve me well. With my Fire Department career, I would find myself waking up most days to go work in an environment consumed by negativity. Workplaces are a playground for complainers and Depressing Daryls and Negative Nancies. All that low-vibration stuff. I would wake up feeling good, ready to go, and motivated. Still, as soon as I hit the station and spent some time with co-workers, I would complain. Then the bell went off, and I got a call, so then I was complaining about that. I complained on the way to the call, on the call, and after the call. It reached the point where I was like, *"Let me stop because what am I complaining about? This is my job."* I knew I had to come to work. I knew I had the power to set the day how I wanted it to go, not taking on other people's emotions, thoughts, and beliefs because in the end, what was I complaining about? Honestly, I was just blowing hot air to feel relatable to others around me.

It's that saying that misery loves company. It's so easy to gravitate toward that energy if you are unconscious about it, and then you wake up. *"Let me stop that because my day is not that bad. My circumstances are not that bad."* Suppose it is getting me to a point where I am not progressing or am unhappy. In that case, there is a 100% chance that I can change my circumstances. Instead of projecting things to people who cannot help you anyway or honestly don't care, how about you go inward and find out what the real issue is and choose to change it? I think, as human beings, we feel safer conforming to the masses. We adapt to other people's ways of thinking, starting in school. We go through a curriculum, but the subjectivity of that teacher heavily influences the curriculum. It also comes from our parents and how we are raised. Our limiting beliefs are ingrained in us very early by what our parents and other authority figures tell us. As a child, you don't have much control over that but as you become an adult, you begin to realize some of the things you were told as a child just doesn't make any damn sense, AT ALL. Also as an adult, with adult responsibilities what you were told as a child no longer serves you anyway. Then our society stays so plugged into the media and the fear of missing out that we want to see what everyone is doing and not doing. Even down to trends with fashion, hair, and the top 10 ways to wear a ponytail. Other people's standards, perceptions, and thought processes influence adults to almost a zombified state. In the workplace, in academia, in religion, even in casual conversation, it's so much more comfortable to adopt someone else's thoughts and opinions than to tap into your own thinking power. British philosopher Bertrand Russel once said, *"A lot of people would rather die than to think, in the face, most do."*

Why do so many people rather conform to what everyone else is saying, believing, and doing? It's because of fear. *"If I say what I feel or act how I feel, what will people say about me?"* People become crippled based on fear of what they think others will say about them. I have always been the type to question the credibility of all who set the standards and create the rules everyone else is supposed to follow. Who gave you the authority to tell me what is right or wrong or what I am not supposed to do or think, or if I make this decision, it is the wrong decision?

When you come into your self-belief and confidence, you realize these people are not any different than you. They are not much smarter than you, and vice versa. You have to be mindful and reinforce taking control of your thoughts everyday. It's a daily activity like bathing. It takes work to master a positive mindset. You must build it through discipline, habit, and conscious thinking. Treat it like a muscle and put in the work everyday just like if you were working out to manage your weight daily. You have to work toward building the muscle of choosing positive thoughts and rejecting negative ones. Some days are much harder than others, especially in business, there are times when it seems I have stalled. I do not see the results from the goals I have set. That's usually an opportunity to stop and check myself because I know I'm often impatient with the process, and that is the time I have to realign with faith and trust the process. The harvest always arrives at perfect timing. It's my job to remain consistent and persist forward.

THE LESSON

For some reason, there's a belief among the masses that the world owes them something, often leading to a victim mindset. If you are always in a victim mode then your direction in life will continuously lead you down a path where not so good things will happen to you. You feel like life is happening to you and not for you. Somebody else is responsible for fixing or improving it, or somebody is doing something to you. A victim mentality does not allow for the accountability you have to take over yourself to elevate and take ownership of your life. Taking ownership is difficult because it sits you face to face with the things you need to improve and take inventory of to become a better person. Now I know that sounds harsh because things happen in life that you cannot control. Still, if something negative, detrimental, or dramatic happens to you in your life, to remain a victim for that, in my opinion, is not going to set you on the trajectory of being victorious. The victorious mindset is to say, *"You know what? I am going to push through. I am not going to sit here and wait for someone to save me,"* or *"I am not going to wait for someone to dictate what my life journey should be or control me in any way. I am just going to go for it. I am going to do what I need to do to heal myself, to educate myself, refine myself, follow my vision and reach my goals."*

If you want to remain in a victim mindset, you must understand what the universe will yield to you. Those will be your results. If you are okay with them, then don't change a thing. But you can't expect other people to remain in that lower vibration with you because, after a while, the universe demands they leave you where you stand to do the work they need to do for their own paths. You cannot get mad at others if or when they choose to improve and refine and you don't. The victorious mindset is where all the magic happens and where all the those who transform their lives and reach success dwell.

THE WIN

It's imperative to understand how powerful your mindset is. There is a saying, *"It takes the same amount of energy to think big as it does to think small, so why not just think big?"* Our subconscious mind is not our thinking mind. It accepts everything we show and tell it so the question is, why is it so much easier to gravitate toward the things we don't want or talk about the things that upset us? Why is it so difficult to talk about what we want, what makes us feel good, what we seek, our desires, and our goals? Because again, our subconscious mind does not know the difference between what is real and what is imagined, and all of our creation starts in our subconscious where our thoughts turn to feelings and our feelings lead to action to bring about the things. What we plant there eventually manifests to the material, so it is important to affirm yourself and spend time working on your victorious mindset muscle daily. When we plant more and more positives, it replaces the negative. It is our God given superpower. It is what separates us from all other species on earth. We are co-creators of our life and have full control over how we shape it into form through proper use of our mindset. Whether you use it appropriately or inappropriately is up to you.

MINDSET CHECK

Most times, you will subscribe to other people's thought processes to feel relatable or because you do not want people to treat you differently because you think outside the box. You're going along to get along, agreeing with others all the while you're thinking to yourself what they're saying is some bullshit and your intuition is telling you to stop picking up what they are putting down. Still, you go along, and when your personal results show up in an unfavorable way, the first thing you want to do is blame it on other people. You subscribe to the limiting beliefs and negative thoughts of others then you play the blame game for how things show up in your life. That's the victim mentality and really you just need to own it. Accept, "I had no business spending that much time talking about this" or "I had no business even being there with these people. Let me not do that again, lesson learned." That is a victorious mindset. That is how winners own their results.

Having a victorious mindset is key to winning in life. When you approach any endeavor with an attitude of confidence, optimism, tenacity, and all the pillars discussed in this book, you set yourself up for achievement. Viewing challenges as opportunities rather than obstacles allows you to grow through difficult situations and become the highest, grandest vision of yourself. Maintaining focus on your goals and visualizing success helps motivate you to keep pushing forward, even when faced with setbacks. A winning mindset means never giving up in the face of adversity, but rather continuing to believe in yourself and your abilities. It is understanding that failures or mistakes are part of the process, not a reflection on your worth. With self-belief, faith, and resilience, you can overcome any hurdles in your way. If you truly feel you can and will prevail, your mindset becomes a self-fulfilling prophecy enabling you to accomplish great things and win at whatever you pursue. Approaching life with a victorious mindset puts success within your grasp.

SNOB-VERB

"I check my mindset more than I check my phone."

THE LAST WORD

"Decide what type of life you want, then say no to everything that doesn't align with it." — *Bianca Wise* —

In closing, I hope you catch that this book not only provides a comprehensive knowledge of taking control of your mindset and harnessing the power of positive thinking to achieve your goals, but that you also gain small but powerful steps you can apply right now to level up. By cultivating a life philosophy and standard of confidence, individuality, visualization, gratitude, solitude, focus, faith, resilience, and good habit forming, you can overcome obstacles, turn challenges into opportunities, and unlock your full potential. You may ask what I think is the most important topic discussed. Well I'm glad you asked because I am going to tell you: It's the imagination.

Have you ever considered the fact that children have all the imagination in the world, but the imagination of adults seemingly diminishes? As we grow up and become adults, our imaginations are often compromised as the world conditions us toward logic and reason. Still, as adults, understanding the power of imagination and how it leads to manifestation is critical for our overall evolution. While it is certain logic, reason, and practicality are critical to our survival and success, we must equally resolve to nurture the innate power of our imagination. We must resolve to exercise it. We must resolve to embrace it. We must resolve to preserve it.

Imagination is the cornerstone of innovation. Many of the most notable advancements–from the invention of the traffic light to the creation of the cell phone and the internet–were products of the imaginative minds of those who dared to innovate. When we consider a world beyond the present reality, one that supersedes what we see in our immediate environments and one that feels impossible to attain, real change happens. It is in this space that our wildest dreams are cultivated and the impossible becomes possible. By harnessing our imaginative thinking, we possess the ability to wonder without restriction, to exist outside of the box, to question the status quo, all while masterminding solutions to the challenges we face.

Our imagination literally has the power to make us and the world around us better. Empathy and understanding are byproducts of a healthy imagination. They enable us to put ourselves in the position of others and to see the world from myriad perspectives. We are also empowered to connect with people on a deeper level. Our levels of empathy are strengthened. In this space, we have the capacity to explore and embrace diverse experiences, cultures, and even stories. It is with open minds that we have the power to become global citizens and to see the wonders of the world while witnessing the greatness that lies within. A healthy imagination has the potential to fuel personal growth and self-discovery. We can set ambitious goals; confront fears; overcome obstacles; and discover the highest, grandest versions of ourselves.

Preserving and nurturing the imagination we are born with is not optional if you aspire to new levels and higher heights. Imagination is among the most powerful tools in your arsenal for personal, professional, and societal growth. If you remember nothing else that I have shared with you amidst the pages of this book, never forget that the future belongs to the dreamers and visionaries who dare to imagine what does not yet exist. Imagination is the spark that ignites revolutions, innovations, and advancements that shape tomorrow. Those who harness its power hold the world in their minds and need only the other pillars discussed in this book to bring their visions into being. The greatest disruptors of the status quo all shared one common trait—the audacity to imagine. Their example challenges us to dream bigger, to envision the future we want, and to never stop reaching for more than the mind believes is possible. For those brave enough to tap into its full potential, imagination is not just the key to success, but the key to mastering yourself. Once you master yourself then you can master the world. See you at the top, mindset snobs!

PLAYLIST

1.   Heavy D — We Got our own thang
2.   Salt & Peppa — Express yourself
3.   Biggie Smalls — Sky's the limit
4.   Mary J. Blige — Just Fine
5.   Shining Star — Earth Wind Fire
6.   I Like That — Janelle Monae
7.   Roar — Katy Perry
8.   Im That Girl — Beyonce
9.   Happy — Pharrell
10. Moment 4 Life — Nicki Minaj
11. Live Your Life — TI/Rihanna
12. So Ambitious — JayZ
13. Winner's Circle — 50 Cent
14. Millionaire — Rick Ross & Lil Wayne
15. A Million Dreams — Pink
16. Everything I Am — Kanye
17. Superstar — Lupe Fiasco
18. Love Yourself — Billy Porter
19. God in Me — Mary Mary
20. Can't Nobody Hold Me Down — Puff Daddy/Mase

AFFIRMATIONS

- I win just by thinking different from most.
- I've got big shit to do. I can't pretend to be average.
- I reflect and refine daily.
- I am intentional with my time, energy, and focus.
- I am so happy and grateful for every step on my journey, both the wins and the lessons.
- I am unapologetic in my evolution.
- I dream it, then real-life it,
- My mindset is my superpower.
- My confidence is fueled by self-belief, not validation of others.
- I'm highly trained in the art of doing me.
- Everything is always working out for me and my greatest good.
- I always and abundantly show up as the best version of me.
- I am purposeful and intentional. Access to me is a privilege.
- Discipline is mastery of yourself. When you master yourself, you master the world.
- Confidence is the audacity to not be defined.
- Individuality is being fully aware of your magic and needing no validation from a single person.
- Everything starts with me.
- Your opinion of me is none of my damn business.

- May your mindset shift the whole damn universe.
- When your heart keeps leading you back to that vision, you have to believe in yourself and go for it.
- Strive to be consistent, not perfect.
- More focus on who you're inspiring, less care about who it's triggering.
- You're not placed on this earth to make others comfortable.
- Choose your own hard, not someone else's thoughts of hard.
- Check your mindset more than you check your phone.
- I get whatever TF I want because I work hard and give this world good energy.
- Trust the process, even when it seems it's not processing.
- When you mind your damn business, the entire universe opens up to you.
- Do what you're called to do so you can stop having an attitude every day.
- Watching yourself grow becomes your favorite show.
- Be great in the mirror first and then in the marketplace.
- If you don't separate yourself from your distractions, your distractions will separate you from your wins.
- The number one way to succeed is to not worry about what everyone else is doing.
- Never quit your daydream.
- Decide what type of life you want, then say no to everything that doesn't align with it.
- Your biggest flex will require solitude.
- Never change your vibe to fit in.
- If the only prayer you said was "Thank You," that would be enough.
- You have to undoubtedly believe in yourself no matter what cards you're dealt.

- Solitude puts you at peace and prepares you to change everything.
- You can never go wrong with staying out the way.
- Confidence is knowing there's no need to compare yourself to anyone else.
- Self-belief is magical.
- Gratitude is gangsta.
- The life you want is on the other side of all the stuff you don't want to do.
- Individuality is the ultimate position of power.
- If it's not paying you, don't mind it.
- Heavy on the faith. Less on the doubt.
- Solitude is self-care.
- Faith is the energy to keep pushing.

BIANCA WISE

Founder and CEO of The Mindset Snob
Author of The Mindset Snob
President of Home Helpers Home Care – Baltimore

Brand Champion Awardee - Home Helpers 2019
President's Club Awardee - Home Helpers 2022
Home Care Pulse Provider of Choice Award 2022.
Caring Star of Excellence Award 2022 & 2023.
2022 Entreprenista 100, Biggest Impact Awardee.

In March 2003, Bianca Wise wrote a sticky note to herself. The note was scribbled with the words "I will be promoted to lieutenant within 10 years". She placed the note in her locker at Baltimore County Fire Department and it was a statement she looked at every single day. With her vision, intentional thoughts, and elevation of mindset, it took Bianca only 9 years to achieve this goal. The first African American Woman to achieve such status in a world predominantly overpowered with white males. But this was not the end of her story, or even the beginning.

Born and raised in Baltimore City, in a single parent family, Bianca had an imagination that would often catapult her into a magical world of unicorns and fairies. A world she created and believed, and one her mom never put a limit on. Being brought up with the freedom to imagine, with no limitations, were the foundations of a successful business woman, and the beginnings of The Mindset Snob.Growing up with the childhood dream of one day becoming an epidemiologist,

Bianca had already written the next part of her journey. Albeit she didn't follow the exact route of becoming a doctor, but the seed of being a leader in helping others was sown. After graduating from high school, Bianca studied nursing at college. However, in a brave move, Bianca changed direction and got a job working with the Federal Government. To be employed with the FBI Headquarters, an environment surrounded by prominent leadership at such a young age, was surreal and inspiring. A few years later, just after 9/11, a time that made many people take stock of their life, Bianca knew there was something else for her in this world. To leave a job with such security and promise was unconventional. But, being someone who lives life as her authentic self through her own vision, Bianca changed course. With the FBI now cemented as an important part of Bianca's story, she began working in the emergency department of a local hospital in Baltimore. Trauma and a fast-paced, quick-thinking environment got her wanting more, and importantly, got her wanting to give more. Working in the emergency department piqued interest around the work of 1st responders, and led to wanting to learn more about EMS altogether. She joined a volunteer fire department, and completed training to become a Paramedic. Another inspiring element to this woman and a course of action that landed her the job as a paramedic firefighter with the Baltimore County Fire Department. This was to become the setting of the "sticky note" and the first test in the power of mindset. Being part of the service for almost 20 years, both as a paramedic firefighter and lieutenant, in an environment known to be challenging for women and for race, Bianca was determined to be the change she wanted to see. In 2012, Bianca won the NAACP Trailblazer award for being the first black woman to become a lieutenant in the Baltimore County Fire department. An accomplishment driven by determination, hard work, intentional thoughts, and a positive mindset. A recognition the universe believed she rightly deserved. In 2018, Lieutenant Bianca Wise, had another epiphany that she was destined for even greater than what she thought, and decided she had came to the end of that chapter with her career. It was time to move on. That was it. An overwhelming message that could not be ignored. Being true to herself, Bianca had the courage and strength to resign from her 20-year career with a detailed 3 page letter of resignation. Bianca was continuing to show the universe that she was the leader in her life's path, and that she was a powerhouse worthy of success. A year after her resignation from the fire department, Bianca started her own business; Home Helpers Home Care of Baltimore. The business began from the second bedroom in her house and faced a global pandemic six months later. Bianca's hard work, focus, determination, bootstrapping, and completion of the Women's Entrepreneurship program at Cornell University made the business not only survive through one of the toughest moments in history, but also reach a level of excellence, expanding to the 7 figure business it is today. With her recent acquisition of a second location in Maryland, Bianca Wise has become the successful business woman that she envisioned herself to be. Her success has led to several well deserved recognitions, and her organization has been recognized as one of the top home care agencies in the nation.

With her mindset, or as Bianca likes to put it, "minding her damn business", being the blueprint for success, and one that has guided her through her accomplishments so far. Bianca knew she had something to give and The Mindset Snob was born. "We don't need anything outside of ourselves to achieve success", is a statement Bianca has proven in her life and one she wanted to share. For many, being in tune with their mindset, being able to imagine and intentionally act on their vision and follow their heart, is a skill and trait that doesn't come easy. But The Mindset Snob teaches you to develop discipline, and other personal development practices so it becomes easier. Discipline, merged with confidence in yourself, a deep rooted confidence. One where you believe in yourself 100% of the time, regardless of external pressures, are the true superpower traits of The Mindset Snob. Being able to feel the fear, yet do it anyways, coupled with being bold and always having a damn good fun time along the way, is a skill Bianca Wise has mastered. With this, Bianca has created her 9 pillars to mindset, which her book explains. The Mindset Snob is the first book Bianca has written, and she has had an interesting journey along the way. One from which she has also learned. "You can achieve anything if you put your mind to it". With that, Bianca's plans and expansion of The Mindset Snob are already growing visions in her colourful imagination. To find out more, subscribe to Bianca's mailing list, or follow her on social media.

www.ingramcontent.com/pod-product-compliance
Lightning Source LLC
Chambersburg PA
CBHW071107120626
46546CB00003B/1293